THE WIDE LENS

How can great companies do everything right – identify real customer needs, deliver excellent innovations, beat their competitors to market – and still fail?

The sad truth is that many companies focus too intensely on their own innovations, and then neglect the ecosystems on which their success depends. In our increasingly interdependent world, winning requires more than just delivering on your own promises. It means ensuring that a host of partners – some visible, some hidden – deliver on their promises, too.

In *The Wide Lens*, innovation expert Ron Adner draws on over a decade of research and field-testing to take you on far-ranging journeys, from Kenya to California, from transport to telecommunications, to reveal the hidden structure of success in a world of interdependence.

With new perspectives on triumphs from Amazon and Apple, as well as monumental failures by Michelin and Pfizer, *The Wide Lens* offers a powerful new set of frameworks and tools that will multiply your odds of innovation success.

The Wide Lens will change the way you see, the way you think – and the way you win.

ABOUT THE AUTHOR

Ron Adner has spent the last decade studying the root cause of innovation success and failure. An award-winning professor of strategy at the Tuck School of Business at Dartmouth College, and previously at INSEAD, he is a speaker and consultant to companies around the world. His writing has appeared in the *Wall Street Journal*, the *Financial Times*, *Forbes* and the *Harvard Business Review*.

THE
WIDE
LENS

A NEW STRATEGY FOR INNOVATION

RON ADNER

PORTFOLIO
PENGUIN

PORTFOLIO PENGUIN

Published by the Penguin Group
Penguin Books Ltd, 80 Strand, London WC2R 0RL, England
Penguin Group (USA) Inc., 375 Hudson Street, New York, New York 10014, USA
Penguin Group (Canada), 90 Eglinton Avenue East, Suite 700, Toronto, Ontario,
Canada M4P 2Y3 (a division of Pearson Penguin Canada Inc.)
Penguin Ireland, 25 St Stephen's Green, Dublin 2, Ireland
(a division of Penguin Books Ltd)
Penguin Group (Australia), 250 Camberwell Road,
Camberwell, Victoria 3124, Australia (a division of Pearson Australia Group Pty Ltd)
Penguin Books India Pvt Ltd, 11 Community Centre, Panchsheel Park,
New Delhi – 110 017, India
Penguin Group (NZ), 67 Apollo Drive, Rosedale, Auckland 0632, New Zealand
(a division of Pearson New Zealand Ltd)
Penguin Books (South Africa) (Pty) Ltd, Block D, Rosebank Office Park,
181 Jan Smuts Avenue, Parktown North, Gauteng 2193, South Africa

Penguin Books Ltd, Registered Offices: 80 Strand, London WC2R 0RL, England

www.penguin.com

First published in the United States of America by Portfolio/Penguin,
a member of Penguin Group (USA) Inc. 2012
First published in Great Britain by Portfolio Penguin 2012
001

Copyright © Ron Adner, 2012

The moral right of the author has been asserted

Printed in Great Britain by Clays Ltd, St Ives plc

A CIP catalogue record for this book is available from the British Library

ISBN: 978–0–670–92168–3

www.greenpenguin.co.uk

MIX
Paper from
responsible sources
FSC
www.fsc.org FSC™ C018179

Penguin Books is committed to a sustainable
future for our business, our readers and our planet.
This book is made from Forest Stewardship
Council™ certified paper.

ALWAYS LEARNING   **PEARSON**

To my students, who have made the journey so rewarding.

And to my family, who have made it possible.

CONTENTS

THE WIDE LENS

Introduction

This book is about the difference between great innovations that succeed and great innovations that fail. It is about the blind spots that undermine great managers in great companies even if they identify real customer needs, deliver great products, and beat their competition to market. It is about why, with ever greater frequency, your success depends not just on your ability to execute your own promises but also on whether a host of partners—some visible, some hidden—deliver on their promises too.

The innovation blind spot is everybody's problem: whether you are a CEO or project team member; in a large multinational or an emergent start-up; in the corporate sector or at a nonprofit; contributing to a collaborative effort or investing in one. No matter your situation, your success depends not just on your own efforts but also on the ability, willingness, and likelihood that the partners that make up your innovation ecosystem succeed as well.

This book offers a new perspective—a wide lens—with which to assess your strategy. It introduces a new set of tools and frameworks that will expose your hidden sources of dependence. It will help you make better choices, take more effective actions, and multiply your odds of success.

The Innovation Blind Spot and Avoidable Failure

Execution focus—developing customer insight, building core competencies, and beating the competition—has become the touchstone of business strategy. In myriad books, lectures, meetings, and workshops, the message to managers is to focus on linking their strategy and their operations, on aligning their teams, on monitoring their competitive environment, and on revitalizing their value propositions. This, they are told, is critical for success.

Yes. Great execution is critical—it is a necessary condition for success. But it is not enough. While this execution focus draws

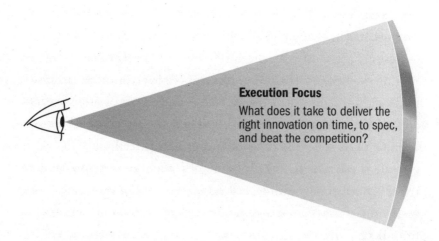

Execution Focus
What does it take to deliver the right innovation on time, to spec, and beat the competition?

Figure I.1: The traditional focus on execution.

attention to unquestionably important parts of a company's environment—its management, employees, owners, customers, and competitors—it creates a blind spot that hides key dependencies that are equally important in determining success and failure.

Philips Electronics fell victim to this blind spot when it spent a fortune to pioneer high-definition television (HDTV) sets in the mid-1980s. The company's executives drove a development effort that succeeded in creating numerous breakthroughs in television technology, offering picture quality that customers loved and that the competition, at the time, could not match. Yet, despite sterling execution and rave reviews, Philips's high-definition TV flopped. Even the most brilliant innovation cannot succeed when its value creation depends on other innovations—in this case the high-definition cameras and transmission standards necessary to make high-definition TV work—that fail to arrive on time. Philips was left with a $2.5 billion write-down and little to show for its pioneering efforts by the time HDTV finally took off twenty years later.

Sony suffered from a similar blind spot, winning a pyrrhic victory as it raced to bring its e-reader to market before its rivals, only to discover that even a great e-reader cannot succeed in a market where customers have no easy access to e-books. And Johnson Controls, which developed a new generation of electrical switches and sensors that could dramatically reduce energy waste in buildings and deliver substantial savings to occupants, discovered that unless and until architects, electricians, and a host of other actors adjusted their own routines and updated their own capabilities, the value of its innovations would never be realized.

In all these cases, smart companies and talented managers invested, implemented, and succeeded in bringing genuinely brilliant innovations to market. But after the innovations launched, they failed. The companies understood how their success depends on meeting the needs of their end customers, delivering great innovation, and beating the competition. But all three fell victim to the innovator's blind spot: failing to see how their success also depended on partners who themselves would need to innovate and agree to adapt in order for their efforts to succeed.

Welcome to the world of innovation ecosystems—a world in which the success of a value proposition depends on creating an alignment of partners who must work together in order to transform a winning idea to a market success. A world in which failing to expand your focus to include your entire ecosystem will set you up for failure. *Avoidable* failure.

Innovation, Expectations, and Reality

Every year, the calls for new innovation to safeguard economic growth, technological progress, and general prosperity grow louder. Every year, vast amounts of money, time, attention, and effort are spent to introduce productive change. From new products and services, to new technologies and business models, to new personnel assessment systems and incentive programs, to new government policies, new education initiatives, and new reporting procedures, innovation initiatives blanket our lives and organizations.

How can we increase profitable growth? Innovate! How can we become more efficient and reduce waste? Innovate! How can we improve loyalty and increase customer satisfaction? Innovate! Innovation is a problem for everyone because it is held up as the solution for everything.

But, despite the excitement, energy, and hype, successful innovation remains the exception rather than the rule. According to surveys by the Product Development and Management Association (PDMA), approximately one out of four new product development efforts ever reach the stage of commercial launch. And even within this highly screened group, 45 percent fail to meet their profit objectives.

Despite these odds, innovation remains imperative. In a world of aggressive competition and easily bored customers, innovation is not a choice but a necessity. A 2010 study by the Boston Consulting Group (BCG) found that 72 percent of senior executives cited innovation-led growth as one of their top three strategic priorities. And if you listen to government leaders and nonprofit heads, you know that their chorus of calls for innovation is deafening. The challenge, then, is to understand the causes of innovation failure and to find ways of increasing effectiveness and safeguarding success.

The experts—authors, gurus, academics, consultants, CEOs—tend to fall into two schools of thought in explaining the sources of failure and the path to success. The first school argues that most innovation failures are rooted in a shortfall in customer insight. Introducing a genuinely new product or service is not enough; if customers don't see the innovation as uniquely valuable, or are unwilling to pay the required price, then the innovation will not succeed. Success, they argue, requires a better way to generate the really good ideas that customers will embrace.

The second school argues that failure is rooted in shortcomings of leadership and implementation. They claim that the key to success lies in building better capabilities for execution and implementation that will enable us to deliver on our promises and beat the competition.

Both perspectives are crucial to understanding and achieving successful innovation. But, even taken together, they are incomplete. Every serious manager today has been inculcated in the mantra of "listen to the voice of the customer" and "focus on execution." And yet, innovation success remains as elusive as ever. Even when firms come up with great new ideas and follow them up with great implementation, failure is not only possible but likely. How can we do better?

Seeing the Hidden Traps

As the long history of failed innovation efforts shows, overlooking your blind spots often leads to tragedy. Good people work hard but ultimately waste their time on initiatives that won't succeed— not because they are less innovative than their competitors or because they can't execute on their project, but because their innovation ecosystem won't come together. If they had the tools to see and understand how their success depends on others, they would have done things differently.

This book is designed to help managers, leaders, and everyone concerned with innovation see their hidden dependencies and understand how to develop robust strategies that are more likely to succeed. To start, you must consider two distinct types of risk that arise within ecosystems: *Co-innovation Risk*, the extent to which the success of your innovation depends on the successful commercialization of other innovations; and *Adoption Chain Risk*, the extent to which partners will need to adopt your innovation before end consumers have a chance to assess the full value proposition.

Choosing to focus on the ecosystem, rather than simply on the immediate environment of innovation, changes everything— from how you prioritize opportunities and threats, to how you think about market timing and positioning, to how you define and measure success. This new paradigm asks innovators to consider the entire ecosystem by broadening their lens to develop a clearer view of their full set of dependencies. To be sure, great customer insight and execution are still vital. But they are only necessary— not sufficient—conditions for success.

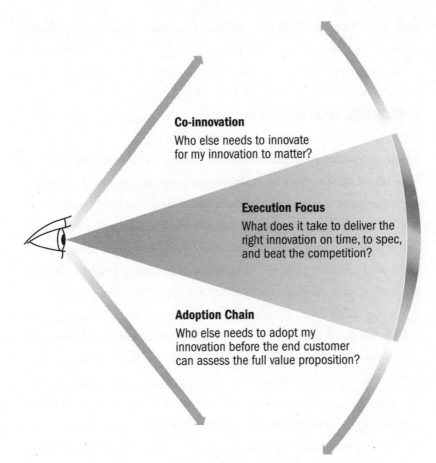

Figure I.2: The wide-lens perspective on innovation strategy.

How We Got Here

The need for collaborative innovation has defined progress since the Industrial Revolution—the lightbulb on its own was a miraculous invention but needed the development of the electric power network to turn it into a profitable innovation. What has changed is the way the collaboration is organized. The shift toward innovation ecosystems follows a historical trend toward greater complexity

and interaction that has characterized the rise of the modern economy. In the beginning, the dominant approach was to house all
this complexity within a single firm—the vertically integrated
organization. In the early days of the twentieth century, vertically
integrated companies like Ford, GE, BASF, and IBM showed that
large size, reduced variable cost, and dedicated research could
produce outstanding change. But while vertical integration offered
control, it required massive investments and led to huge, unwieldy
organizations. At the close of the twentieth century, firms like Toyota, Dell, and Nestlé led their industries by learning how to leverage external supply chains to outsource activities, reduce fixed
costs, and increase operational flexibility, setting a new benchmark
for competitiveness that their rivals struggled to meet.

At the beginning of each management innovation wave, the
first firms to master the principles of the new approach—from
assembly-line manufacturing in the 1920s to management information systems in the 1950s to relational contracting, just-in-time
inventories, and total quality management in the 1990s—enjoyed
a substantial competitive advantage. Rival firms looked on in awe,
trying to figure out what magic allowed for such vastly superior
results. But as these innovation strategies diffused more broadly
across organizations, their mastery stopped being a source of differentiation and became, instead, simply an operational requirement for getting in the game.

Today we are witnessing another transition point. The enormous benefits that accrued to firms who mastered supply chain
management—global procurement, just-in-time-production, lean
inventory management—are still real, but they are now widely
shared. In industry after industry, we see a major change taking
place as firms shift from using supply chains to offer better products to embracing partnerships and collaboration to offer better

"solutions." It isn't enough for an auto manufacturer to produce a reliable, fast, efficient car: it also needs to offer state-of-the-art computer navigation and entertainment systems. It isn't enough for hardware stores to sell a variety of goods efficiently: they also need to design classes and tutorials so people can learn how to use them. Newspapers must offer both articles and videos; marketers must offer both advertising campaigns and user communities; phones must offer not just voice calling but an entire media experience. Success in this world requires mastery of ecosystem strategy.

There is a growing trend to not go it alone. In a 2011 survey of senior executives by the Corporate Executive Board, 67 percent expected new partnerships, and 49 percent expected new business models, to be critical drivers of their growth in the upcoming five to ten years. And indeed, today's exemplar firms—from Apple in consumer electronics to Amazon in retail, from Roche in pharmaceuticals to Raytheon in defense, and from Hasbro in toys to Turner in construction—do much more than "just" execute flawlessly on their own initiatives. They orchestrate the activities of an array of partners so that their joint efforts increase the value created by their own initiatives many times over. These leaders have understood the nature of the blind spot and have expanded their perspective. They have deployed a wide lens in setting their strategy and prospered in their embrace of the ecosystem opportunity.

The Wide Lens

Luck—good and bad—always plays a role in determining outcomes. But in every postmortem analysis of failure, we uncover two different types of surprises: the ones we couldn't have seen coming and the ones we should have.

All too often we see strategies devolve into tactical adjustments, hurriedly and reactively pursued to compensate for realities that could have been foreseen. The old tools are no longer enough. They may have clarified how to think about customers, competition, and capabilities, but they offer precious little guidance on how to think and act in an interdependent world.

This book will give you a new set of tools with which to craft your strategy and build your success. The ideas in each chapter build on each other, and as you progress, you will increase your understanding, your toolbox, and your odds of success.

In part 1, I introduce the key concepts that make innovating in ecosystems different, beginning with an examination of why excellent managers can become so focused on their own execution that they fail to recognize the extent to which their success depends on others. We will see how co-innovation risk and adoption chain risk combine to create the innovation blind spot and why there is a natural tendency for these problems to stay hidden from view (and correction) until it's too late.

In part 2, we move from analysis to choice in the context of ecosystems. We will explore how to assess alternatives, how to choose positions, and how to think about timing. We will see why a wide-lens perspective fundamentally changes how we decide where to compete, how to compete, and when to compete.

In part 3, we shift from choice to intervention. I will present a set of new strategies for building and shaping ecosystems—how to reconfigure the structure of dependence and how to leverage advantage within and across ecosystems. We will see how the wide-lens toolbox can be credibly deployed to avoid needless failures and multiply your odds of success.

Dependence is not becoming more visible, but it is becoming more pervasive. What you don't see can kill you. Don't let your blind spot become your downfall.

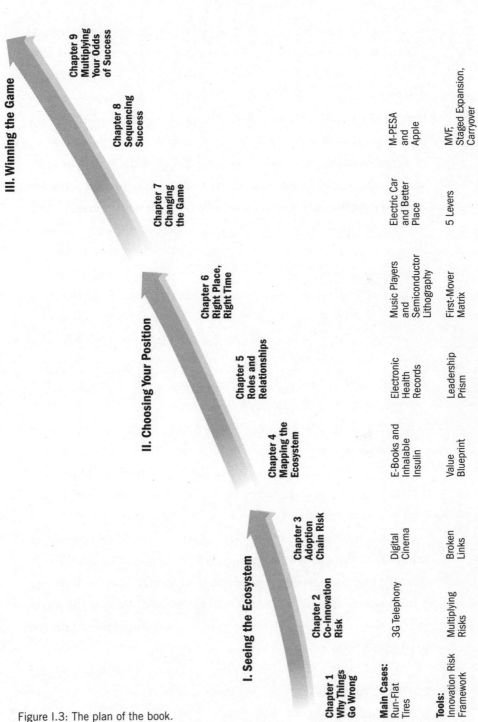

Figure I.3: The plan of the book.

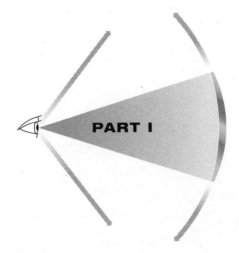

PART I

Seeing the Ecosystem

III. Winning the Game

II. Choosing Your Position

I. Seeing the Ecosystem

Chapter 1
Why Things
Go Wrong

Chapter 2
Co-innovation
Risk

Chapter 3
Adoption
Chain Risk

Main Cases:
Run-Flat
Tires

3G Telephony

Digital
Cinema

Tools:
Innovation Risk
Framework

Multiplying
Risks

Broken
Links

Why Things Go Wrong When You Do Everything Right

Like a drumbeat, the mantra of success echoes through the halls of every organization: (1) "Put the customer first," (2) "Deliver on your promise," and (3) "Do a better job than the competition." Each individual directive presents a formidable organizational challenge, but serious managers know that the real challenge lies in satisfying all three requirements simultaneously.

A great idea that excites your organization but not your customer creates no value. A great idea that you cannot implement is a theoretical dream. And a great idea that you implement, but which the competition implements better, is at best a disadvantaged effort and at worst a waste of both time and resources.

So what should we expect if we pull off the miracle and combine a great idea and great execution? In a world of stand-alone projects, where outcomes are determined by how well you and your team deliver on your initiative, the answer is success. But over the past two decades we have witnessed a systematic shift away from independent success. As customers get bored and competitors catch up, firms are trying to break out of the commodity trap by finding ways to leverage products and services provided by other partners to drive their own success.

More and more, managers and executives are being pushed into a world of greater collaboration. The upside is that, by working in concert with others within and across organizations, you can accomplish greater things with greater efficiency than you could ever accomplish alone. The downside, however, is that your success now depends not just on your own efforts but on your collaborators' efforts as well. Greatness on your part is not enough. You are no longer an autonomous innovator. You are now an actor within a broader innovation ecosystem. Success in a connected world requires that you manage your dependence. But before you can manage your dependence, you need to see it and understand it. Even the greatest companies can be blindsided by this shift.

Michelin's Run-Flat Saga

In the early 1990s, Michelin was in an enviable position. Best in class by a host of measures and an industry leading brand (who can forget the iconic Michelin Man?), the company was not only the largest tire maker in the world but also the most innovative.

With a long history of successful innovations stretching back to its beginnings in the late 19th century, Michelin was always looking for new opportunities to create value and grow.

In 1992, a small group of Michelin executives conducted a breakout session. The goal? To come up with the next big innovation, one that would spur sales, grow profits, and redefine the way consumers would think about tires. The result—the PAX System— was an idea so good, so powerful, that it launched Michelin on an ambitious path to transform the entire tire industry. "The PAX System is our biggest technological breakthrough since we patented the radial tire in 1946," the company proudly announced. "In simple terms, we have reinvented the tire."

The PAX System was a run-flat tire that would continue to "run flat" and not sacrifice performance even if punctured. If you suffered a blowout with run-flat tires, you could continue to drive as if nothing had happened. No need for an emergency pull-over. No need to get out the spare tire and jack from the trunk. And no need to call a tow truck and wait by the side of the road until help finally arrived.

Instead, a light on your dashboard would let you know a puncture had occurred and that you could drive for another 125 miles, at up to 55 mph, before having to pull into a garage to get the tire repaired affordably and efficiently. Here was a truly great innovation—one that would make customers' lives easier and safer, while driving new profitable growth for the company. "The adoption of the PAX System is inevitable," declared Thierry Sortais, the PAX project director, summing up Michelin's expectations. High expectations indeed!

Michelin saw the run-flat as a revolutionary growth engine not only for the company but for the entire tire industry. Despite the importance of tires—"the single most important component on a vehicle," according to *Motor Trend* magazine—the tire industry was brutally competitive, marked by overcapacity and low margins. Making things worse, the majority of drivers did not differentiate among tires, regarding one brand as good as another, and therefore chose their tires largely on the basis of price.

A half century earlier, Michelin had commercialized the radial tire, a breakthrough innovation that dramatically increased tread life, safety, and fuel efficiency. The radial turned Michelin into a world leader and forever changed the tire and automobile industries. PAX was Michelin's chance to do it again.

By traditional standards, Michelin executed brilliantly on a well-thought-out innovation strategy. Market research showed overwhelming customer support for the product's value proposition, and Michelin had everything in place to succeed. The company had assembled a team of its best researchers, designers, and engineers and gave them top priority for resources and support. And the competition could not keep up. Not only were rival approaches to run-flat tires inferior to Michelin's PAX System in terms of reliability, functionality, comfort, and safety, but the fortress of patents that Michelin had assembled around the system ensured that no competitor could enter the market with an imitative offer. Indeed, Michelin's offer was so compelling that the company was able to co-opt its main rivals to support the PAX System as an industry standard.

But in the end, despite brilliant execution, the PAX story is one of failure. Because when your success depends on others, as it did for Michelin, *execution is not enough.*

Why Everything Looked So Right

Before we can understand why Michelin failed, we have to understand where it succeeded.

Seeing the Unmet Need

Michelin's extensive market research showed that flat tires were both prevalent (60 percent of U.S. drivers had experienced a flat tire over a five-year period) and dangerous (in the U.S. alone nearly 250,000 automotive accidents per year were due to low tire pressure). If Michelin could eliminate the danger of underinflated tires and flats—both of which PAX did—it would represent a giant leap in consumer safety.

Michelin's partners were also enthusiastic about the idea. Automakers liked the PAX System's improved safety, which they could leverage as a key differentiator for new vehicles. But even more exciting were the new design possibilities run-flats offered. By eliminating the need for a bulky spare tire, Michelin's system gave automakers the freedom to innovate for themselves by creating roomier car interiors.

Initial discussions with service garages suggested that they were also enthusiastic about the prospect of repairing run-flat tires. They could charge customers higher prices for repairing the tire, enjoying higher margins while maintaining service volumes (the PAX System would not reduce the number of punctured tires—it would only eliminate their danger and inconvenience).

Indeed, the PAX tires fit neatly into a modern timeline of strong safety features. Since the 1960s, vehicles had seen a steady of stream of breakthrough safety innovations—antilock brakes, traction control, crumple zones, and air bags—that first debuted on high-end vehicles and gradually became mainstream components. Michelin was positioning PAX System tires to be the next in line. CEO Édouard Michelin, great-grandson and namesake to the company's nineteenth-century founder, was a champion of the PAX System: "We consider it a major development in vehicle safety, as important as the introduction of radials, if not more important."

The PAX System was not the first attempt to tackle the problem of flat tires. Over the years, Goodyear, Bridgestone, and Michelin itself had all introduced self-supporting tires (SSTs) that incorporated reinforced sidewalls to support the weight of the car in the event of a flat. But SSTs had always suffered from significant drawbacks. The added weight of the reinforced sidewalls reduced fuel efficiency, and their rigidity led to a harsh, stiff ride. And the maximum range of punctured SSTs was only around fifty miles. As a result, SSTs' share of the tire market was less than 1 percent. Clearly, there was plenty of room for improvement. The PAX System was a completely new approach.

Moving to Execution

PAX System development started in earnest in early 1993. In contrast to the clunky SSTs, the PAX System's unique architecture offered an elegant solution that sacrificed nothing in performance, nothing in weight, and provided twice the range of the

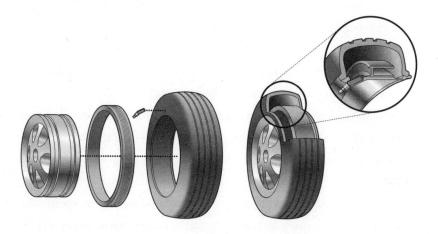

Figure 1.1: The four components of the PAX System: wheel, inner support ring, tire pressure monitor, and tire.

existing alternative. Michelin's engineers came up with a novel (and heavily patented) four-in-one combination of tire, support ring, alloy wheel, and tire pressure monitor.

Unlike traditional tires, which are held in place against the wheel by air pressure, in the PAX System the wheel was physically clamped onto the tire. Thus, in the event of a loss of air pressure, the tire would stay connected to the rim, riding on the inner support ring. The tire might look flat from the outside, but vehicle performance would be unaffected. Sitting in the driver's seat, the motorist would not feel a difference.

The PAX System was a radical product change, but it required even more radical organizational changes within Michelin to become a reality. Traditionally, tire companies (like Michelin) made tires; rim manufacturers made metal wheels; and the two were assembled by the auto manufacturers. With the PAX System, Michelin had to oversee the design and production of an integrated system. The support ring, which would need to bear the weight of the car in the case of a flat, presented an enormous material science challenge. The wheels themselves needed to be asymmetric to allow for both the support ring and the necessary clamping mechanism. Finally, the tire pressure monitoring system, with its sensor, control unit, and alarm system, also needed to be developed. Michelin had to shift from product manufacturer to system integrator.

Michelin rose to the challenge. And despite confronting enormous technical challenges internally and among its partners, the company proudly launched the PAX System to the world in early 1998.

Soon after, Michelin took a second decisive step to secure the PAX System's success. Carmakers insist on multiple suppliers for their components. Indeed, this had been a major hindrance to the adoption of radial tires fifty years earlier, and the PAX System would not be an exception. But in strategizing its rollout of PAX, Michelin proactively sought out, and found, partnerships with other tire makers to whom it eagerly licensed the technology. In June of 2000, after a year of secret negotiations, Michelin unveiled its masterstroke: an unprecedented alliance with Goodyear, the world's second-largest tire maker.

"The two companies have decided to collaborate in a joint venture to develop leading-edge technology allowing vehicles to run on flat tires," read the joint statement. "Today, PAX System has become a new standard. Goodyear and Michelin are convinced . . . that PAX System is the best platform for incorporation of future tire concepts into new vehicle designs."

Between them, the two companies controlled almost 40 percent of the global tire market, and both expected the new alliance to open the door to widespread industry adoption.

Expecting Success (2001–07)

As 2001 began, widespread adoption of PAX System technology no longer seemed a question of *if* but *when*. J.D. Power & Associates performed its annual survey asking consumers what they put at the top of their priority list for automotive features: seven out of eight consumers chose run-flats.

The first company to sign on was Mercedes, which began equipping its ultra-high-end Class S armored cars with the tires. Cadillac soon announced it would start equipping select Corvette models. And in February, Renault, the French carmaker, launched the first production-line vehicle with PAX run-flats: the Renault Scenic. There were dozens of other development projects in the works with all the major automakers.

Discussing the benefits of PAX in 1999, Michelin CFO Eric

Bourdais le Charbonniere remarked, "They perform better in every respect. In ten years, there won't be any other kind of tire except PAX."

Michelin moved quickly over the next two years. It struck additional deals with Audi and Rolls-Royce to stock run-flats on models in the United States, Australia, and Europe. And it added the fourth- and ninth-largest tire makers in the world, Sumitomo Rubber Industries and Toyo Tire & Rubber Company, to its PAX alliance. The new members provided a strong entry into Asia and opened up future deals with carmakers based there.

By the end of 2004, J.D. Power & Associates had come out with a new survey predicting that by 2010 more than 80 percent of cars would be fitted with run-flats.

In the United States, Honda announced that beginning in 2005 it would equip its best-selling Odyssey minivan with PAX tires. According to a Honda spokesperson, "The bottom-line benefit for the customers is the security of never being stuck on the side of the highway. That's an important thing, especially for a minivan buyer who's thinking a lot about safety and security."

To ensure a successful launch, Michelin and Honda embarked on unprecedented coordination. Michelin boosted the standard PAX warranty to cover the first two years of driving or 50 percent of tread wear and began training and certifying Honda dealers and tire dealerships with PAX across the country.

In the rush to market, however, many of the Honda dealers were not ready when the Odyssey was launched. Michelin was aware of the problem. "As more vehicles take to the road with the PAX System, the traditional service and repair networks will continue to grow with them," assured Michelin vice president of marketing Tom Chubb. As we will see, this was little comfort to Odyssey owners with PAX tires.

Confronting Failure

Despite a worldwide alliance of the leading tire manufacturers, and incorporation into popular car models, problems surrounding PAX were mounting, and eroding carmakers' initial enthusiasm. Most pressing among these was growing consumer frustration with the difficulty of finding service centers that could repair the tires. Unable to repair flats, many drivers were forced instead to purchase brand-new tires, often in pairs so as to maintain their vehicles' balance and alignment. At around $300 per tire, the run-flat value proposition was rapidly eroding. Avoiding the danger and inconvenience of a punctured tire was a great proposition when the driver only had to pay a moderate premium for repair, but it was far less compelling when it required the driver to pay hundreds of dollars to replace the entire tire assembly.

In the United States, several class-action lawsuits were filed alleging that Michelin, Honda, and Nissan had "never disclosed that neither they nor any third parties maintained sufficient repair or replacement facilities (or the necessary equipment to perform such repair or replacement)." In November 2007, Michelin formally announced an end to further development of PAX. "Today we do not intend to develop a new PAX simply because there is no big market demand," it said in a statement. "The market demand is insufficient to justify the expense."

What had started as an "inevitable success" ended as a massive corporate write-off. But what makes this case so interesting is that the failure of PAX was not rooted in a misunderstanding of customer needs, in a competence shortfall that led to an inadequate tire, or a loss to a more able competitor. Rather, the failure was due to the inability to deliver the promised value proposition because of an unseen—but fully predictable—problem with the service network.

Michelin's Blind Spot

If the PAX run-flat tire had been a stand-alone tire innovation, its success would have been largely assured by 2001. Historically, tire innovations live or die depending on end-user response. But with the PAX System, end-user acceptance was just one of the necessary conditions for success. The PAX System failed precisely because it was *not* a stand-alone innovation. For it to succeed, other members of Michelin's innovation ecosystem—the car manufacturers and, crucially, the service stations—would need to buy into the system as well. Indeed, end users would be able to assess the attractiveness of the full run-flat value proposition only *after* the rest of the ecosystem embraced the new tire.

Commenting on the slow takeoff of PAX, Michelin director of technical marketing Don Baldwin explained, "This is not unlike the transition to radial from bias years and years ago. That was a relatively slow process, too. The market will determine that. We believe the PAX System will be the standard of the future." But the very structure of the PAX ecosystem dictates its transition would be *entirely* unlike the radial transition. It is here that Michelin's blind spot becomes apparent: to succeed, PAX would require a fundamental transformation in the tire ecosystem.

Tires are sold into two main segments: the replacement market (RM), which makes up three-quarters of industry unit sales, and the original equipment manufacturer (OEM) market, which accounts for the other one-quarter. Tire makers focus huge efforts on winning OEM contracts because they are a strong predictor of RM sales, since most consumers simply replace their old tires with the kind they originally had.

While automaker support provides a boost for new tires, tire makers can also reach consumers directly through the replacement market. Most tire innovations, like the radial tire, succeeded in the replacement market first and were only later able to penetrate the OEM market. Aquatred tires, for example, started as, and remain, a hugely successful replacement market product (see figure 1.2). The SST approach to run-flats, which the PAX System was supposed to dominate (and which the industry continues to pursue) also followed this same traditional path to market.

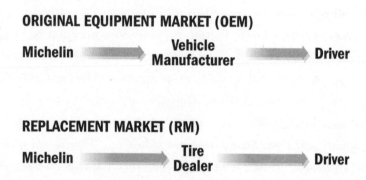

Figure 1.2: Paths to market for stand-alone tire innovations.

The very nature of the PAX System, however, required a different path to market, one which would add new actors and new interactions to the system (see figure 1.3). First, it required automakers to provide a very different level of support than was necessary for traditional new tires. Because of their asymmetric wheels and tire pressure monitoring systems, PAX had to start in the OEM market, as a designed-in feature of a new car. As such, there was no possibility of building initial support in the replacement market. Indeed, in order for run-flats to deliver on their full value proposition, such as by allowing for extra interior space through the elimination of the spare tire, they would need to be included as part of a vehicle's design, long before it was even produced. And since the design-to-production cycle for cars can be well over thirty-six months, this meant that carmakers would have to decide to adopt Michelin's innovation years before consumers would even have a chance to decide whether PAX tires were an attractive option.

Second, it required new car dealers to enter the picture. When carmakers introduce brand-new systems for their cars (think air-conditioning, antilock brakes, power windows and steering, sound system, GPS), they tend to offer them first as optional features, for which buyers pay extra, and only later include them as part of the standard car package. If a feature is part of the standard package, selling the product to customers is easy because all that is needed is carmaker support. But when it becomes an option, a new player is added to the mix: the salesperson at the new car dealership. Now, sales also depend on whether the salesperson is incentivized to guide customers to buy the PAX package for their new car versus, say, a GPS or satellite radio package. And while Michelin had deep experience in dealing with automakers and tire dealers, their relationship with new car dealers was much less established.

Finally, and most critically, PAX required service garages to enter the picture in an entirely new way. For garages, repairing innovative tires had never required any major change to their activities, equipment, or capabilities. For this reason, they were never a factor in the success of new tire launches. But repairing a PAX tire was a different story: the garage needed completely new equipment to clamp and unclamp the tire to and from the wheel, new tools to calibrate the tire pressure monitoring system, and new training for its repair staff. What's more, to ensure correct

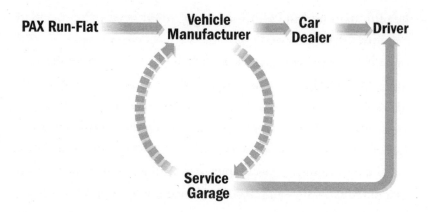

Figure 1.3: Path to market for the PAX run-flat tire innovation.

repairs, Michelin required technicians to undergo a rigorous cer-
tification process to be qualified to service the tire.

Although carmakers, auto dealers, and service garages have
always played a role in the success or failure of tires, the very
nature of the PAX proposition changed this dynamic. In the past,
these players had served only a peripheral role, but with PAX they
became core to delivering the value proposition. Thus, they would
need to be managed in a very different way than ever before.

When the PAX System was developed, it created new interactions not only between Michelin and these players but also among
them. For a carmaker, the attractiveness of installing run-flat tires
on a car depends on how many garages are able to repair the tire
in case of a flat. But the attractiveness for a service garage to install
the repair equipment and train its personnel depends on how
many cars on the road have PAX installed. Even as the PAX System became a standard on a handful of new car models, these
cars were but a trickle into an ocean. It would take many years
before they could possibly account for a meaningful percentage of

cars on the road—and, for this reason, years before they could be meaningfully attractive for garages to service.

Figure 1.3 presents a very different picture of value creation than the one Michelin was used to managing. The contrast with figure 1.2 is striking: new actors are added, old actors eliminated; positions are shifted; and new links and relationships are created. We can see that underlying the PAX value proposition was the requirement of a complete reconfiguration of the tire ecosystem. And this meant that the difference between the success and failure of PAX would hinge on Michelin's ability to see and drive this reconfiguration.

Ecosystem reconfiguration is at the heart of every new value proposition that breaks from the existing industry mold. Keurig and Nespresso combining coffeemakers and single-serve capsules hinged on transforming their relationships with distributors; Caterpillar offering fleet management and remote monitoring and operation of its construction machines hinged on creating new interactions at construction sites; Marriott expanding from hotel rooms to travel packages hinged on the seamless integration of new partners: any organization that aspires to transition from stand-alone products to integrated solutions, from insulated projects to collaborative systems, is signing on to a transformation of this sort. *For these strategies to succeed, it is no longer enough to manage your innovation. Now you must manage your innovation ecosystem.*

For many companies, including Michelin, managing innovation ecosystems is problematic because the tools and systems they have honed over years of managing successful stand-alone innovations are ill suited to address the interdependence challenges that are inherent in the transition to ecosystems. This is the source of the innovation blind spot. And this is exactly what the wide-lens tools and principles introduced in this book will allow you to see and manage.

PAX Run-Flat Epilogue

I feel great sympathy for Michelin's managers. They waged a val-
iant campaign to establish the PAX System as the new tire standard, trying to repeat the company's success with the radial of
fifty years earlier. But the structure of the PAX ecosystem was
entirely different. Most critically, the PAX value proposition created an entirely new role for service garages—one that they were
not eager to assume. Non-adoption by this critical partner was the
key barrier to the PAX System's success. The inability to service
PAX tires led to consumer backlash and lawsuits that, in turn,
reduced automakers' enthusiasm for the system.

Simultaneously, the uniqueness of the PAX offer was being
eroded by the spread of tire pressure monitoring systems (TPMSs).
TPMS had been developed to work with the PAX System. But TPMS
also worked with standard tires. Simply installing an air pressure
monitor (standard on PAX tires but still uncommon in the 1990s)
was expected to reduce blowouts and prevent as many as 79 deaths
and 10,365 injuries each year in the United States alone. And
although the standard installation of pressure monitoring did not
negate the other unique features of the PAX System, it certainly
stood to reduce the PAX System's *relative* advantage. And this
reduced everyone's incentives to keep pursuing the PAX vision—
automakers saw reduced potential to tout it as a safety-based differentiator, and garages saw even less reason to invest in specialized
repair equipment. The window of opportunity had closed.

An Alternative Market

The bottleneck to success in the commercial market was not due
to a lack of driver enthusiasm for the PAX value proposition; it was
that garages kept the value proposition from being realized.

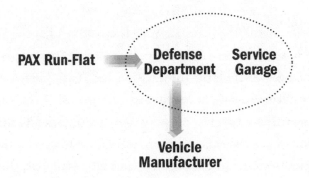

Figure 1.4: PAX in the military market.

Interestingly, a modified version of the PAX System has been an unqualified success in the one market where service stations do not play an independent role: the military. The U.S. Army's fleet of Stryker armored vehicles, introduced into combat service in 2003, are equipped with run-flat tires.

Using a wide lens, we can see that the critical difference was not that flat tires in a war zone are a bigger worry than flat tires at rush hour (although they very clearly are). Rather, the key difference is the structure of dependence:

The structure of the military market (figure 1.4) favors the run-flat's success because there is no intermediary between the buyer (defense department) and Michelin. Instead, the order of events is that first the buyer agrees they want to adopt the system, and then it specifies the kinds of tires it wants on the military vehicles (unlike in the consumer market where the cars are designed for the buyer). And, critically, since the military runs its own garages, the buyer takes care of the service role themselves. Using the wide-lens terminology, in the military market there was much lower adoption chain risk since the customer agrees first, and then the rest of the system follows suit.

As of 2010, over 3,500 Strykers have been built and played prominent roles in the campaigns in Iraq and Afghanistan. As the flagship light armored vehicle for the U.S. military, more are on the way. Unfortunately, the military market alone is not enough to make PAX a success—not because it isn't profitable, but because Michelin's initial expectations were to revolutionize all vehicles on the road, not just the small niche of military transport vehicles. As it is, Michelin's fifteen-year PAX odyssey left them with little but a costly, though valuable, lesson.

Is There a Better Way?

It is always easy to critique failure after the fact, but it is not always fair. An unfair critique focuses on the failure and criticizes management for the outcome. It focuses on the specific choices made. A fair critique focuses on the *way* that choices were made. It offers an approach that could have reasonably been used to arrive at defensible recommendations before the outcomes were known.

The failure of PAX was such a surprising defeat because, from a traditional perspective, Michelin did everything right. The company's mistake was its failure to understand the innovation ecosystem on which its success depended.

In the end, Michelin's failure was rooted in its inability to bring enough service stations on board with the PAX System. But in the beginning, Michelin treated service stations as a low priority. The reason, of course, was history. Historically, service station support could be assumed, but in the run-flat world that Michelin constructed, service stations held the keys. And because Michelin underestimated their role, it underinvested in managing this critical dependence. This was not as much a problem of funding as it was a problem of strategy. When Michelin took the major step of redesigning the entire wheel, the company took on a whole new role without realizing it.

We have been taught the consumer is the final arbiter of value. But the consumer is not the *only* arbiter of value. Often, a host of other partners stand between the innovator and the end consumer, such as the suppliers who need to ship components to your factory, the distributors who navigate your product through the retail channel, and the retail outlets where the end consumer finally decides whether or not to purchase your offer. These partners customize activities for every product launch—new procurement arrangements, new manufacturing, new marketing support, etc. But the ways in which these activities are organized, and the ways in which different partners interact with one another, tend to follow a well-established set of routines. As long as your innovation fits within their routines, these partners remain invisible and your success is determined on a stand-alone basis. But when your innovation depends on these partners to change their routines—as Michelin's PAX System did—they become a critical, but easy to overlook, determinant of your success.

The principles and tools that I will explore in the coming chapters will help ensure that you will not fall into this trap.

Throughout this book, our approach will be to assess the value proposition of every new innovation according to the three risks of innovation:

Execution risk: The challenges you face in bringing about your innovation to the required specifications, within the required time.

Co-innovation Risk: The extent to which the successful commercialization of your innovation depends on the successful commercialization of other innovations.

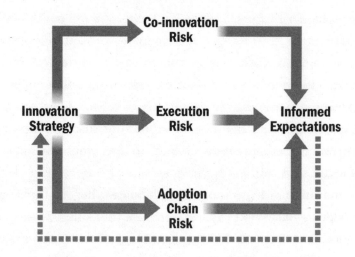

Figure 1.5: The three risks of innovation.

Adoption Chain Risk: The extent to which partners will need to adopt your innovation before end consumers have a chance to assess the full value proposition.

Each of these risks is governed by a different logic. And as we saw in the Michelin saga, success requires that each risk be addressed. Michelin managed its own execution challenges well. It was also successful in navigating its partners' co-innovation challenges (rim manufacturers responsible for developing the new clamping architecture; component suppliers responsible for developing the TPMS solution). Its failure was rooted in mismanaging the adoption risk posed by the hidden assumption in its strategy: that garages would invest in PAX repair equipment in advance of PAX's mass-market adoption.

The traditional tools of strategy, marketing, operations, and project management offer excellent guidance for seeing and managing execution risk, and so I will not focus on those here. These are necessary, but not sufficient, conditions for success. In this book, I will take great ideas and great execution as the starting point and focus on the requirements for success that lie beyond your own initiative. This book is about seeing interaction between your own execution risk and the risks that are introduced by your eco-system partners. It is about how to revisit your strategy to proac-tively manage these interactions and, in this way, drive better outcomes.

Co-innovation risk and adoption chain risk lurk in the blind spot of traditional strategy. They remain dormant as long as your innovations follow established lines. But when you try to break out of the mold of incremental innovation, ecosystem challenges are likely to arise. This is not a problem if you are prepared. It can be devastating if you are not. Just like the blind spot when you are changing driving lanes, not seeing the other car coming doesn't make the accident any less awful. The same is true with strategy: a strategy that does not properly account for the external depen-dencies on which its success hinges does not make those depen-dencies disappear. It just means that you will not see them until it is too late.

In order to avoid these accidents, you need to adopt a struc-tured approach to innovating in ecosystems, a new set of guiding questions to ask when your own efforts no longer determine your success. The following chapters will give you that approach. They will expand your focus beyond the usual (and correct) obsession with customers, capabilities, and competition. They will give you a perspective that will help reveal the dependencies that hide beneath the surface, avoid the predictable disasters, and choose and manage initiatives in a smarter and more effective way.

CHAPTER 2

Co-innovation Risk:

Seeing the Real Odds When You Don't Innovate Alone

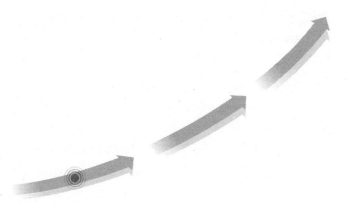

C ollaborate. Cooperate. Co-create. Co-innovate. The calls to leverage the efforts and capabilities of others in order to accelerate the path to profitable growth are growing louder and louder. Organizations across a wide range of industries have discovered new ways to stitch together a complex web of partners and offer superior value propositions to consumers. The ability to create and manage these innovation ecosystems inspires amazement and praise from customers, and admiration and fear among rivals.

For many companies, however, these co-innovation attempts are costly failures, characterized by broken promises and missed expectations. Why? Because when you rely on partners to enable your success, your success becomes vulnerable to your partners' progress. Delays and compromises are more likely to occur when the work depends on cooperation.

Competent managers know that success requires obsessive focus on capabilities, customers, and the competition. But too often they fall victim to the blind spot of *Co-innovation Risk*. While managers have rich processes in place to assess and manage their own execution challenges ("What do I need to do to deliver my project on time, to spec, ahead of the competition?"), they do not fully understand their dependence on their partners' co-innovation challenges ("What are the hurdles facing the other innovations that must come about for my project to succeed?").

Regardless of the nature of the complementary innovation—technological (a better battery for electric cars); procedural (a new quality assurance process, a new service interaction); organizational (an integrated selling approach that combines offers from multiple divisions)—co-innovation risk transforms the odds of success. In this chapter we will use Nokia's journey in 3G telephony to uncover the logic of co-innovation risk, and identify paths to overcome it.

Great Expectations: Telecom in the '90s

The first generation of commercial mobile telephony emerged in the 1980s. An analog network with devices that were bulky, expensive, and slow, it was primarily used by governments, law enforcement, and the military. The second generation of mobile telephony (2G) was rolled out in the early 1990s. Based on digital signals, this new network was much faster and capable of transmitting both voice and small amounts of data, such as Short Message Service (SMS) text messages. The technology of 2G made it both possible and affordable for mainstream consumers to own a small handset that allowed them to call virtually anyone, anytime, from anywhere. After fifteen years of incubation in niche segments, cellular phones had finally hit the mass market.

Figure 2.1: Motorola's DynaTAC 8000x was the world's first portable handheld cellular phone. Introduced in 1983, the phone weighed 1.75 pounds, supported 30 minutes of talk time after 10 hours of charging, and retailed for $3,995. (© *Motorola Mobility, Inc., Legacy Archives Collection. Reproduced with permission.*)

The 1990s were the heyday of mobile telecom. Across the sector all the players—telecom operators, infrastructure providers, and handset makers—were enjoying record growth and profits thanks to one of the largest explosions of technology in history. Nowhere was this more concentrated than in Scandinavia, where two of the largest players, Finland's Ericsson and Sweden's Nokia, lived and competed side by side. Global cell phone use had exploded, and by the year 2000, mobile network operators had over 700 million users around the world.

It was a good time to be at either company, and Jorma Ollila, then CEO of Nokia, presided over an unprecedented wave of growth with sales of mobile systems and handsets growing at 50 percent a year.

But by 1999, leading players across the globe—Nokia and Ericsson in Europe, NEC and Samsung in Asia, and Motorola in the United States—were all bumping up against an unpleasant reality. Customers were beginning to take for granted the incredible technology that allowed for mobile communications, and new rivals were rushing into the space on all sides as barriers to entry fell. In Western Europe the problem was particularly acute. Already almost 70 percent of adults had a mobile phone, which left little room for growth in new customers. How could consumers be convinced not just to trade in their perfectly functional old phones for an updated version, but to be willing to spend significantly more on their next handset? What was Nokia to do to sustain profitable growth?

Nokia's solution, and the industry consensus, was 3G—a third generation of mobile communications that would enable not just voice but streaming data. Proponents envisioned a world in which consumers could talk on their phone, watch video, and conduct mobile commerce. Suddenly, your phone was not just a phone; it was a portable Internet device, capable of connecting you 24/7 to the World Wide Web.

"This next stage in the growth of the communications business will be in the mobile multimedia and location-based services," predicted Keiji Tachikawa, the president of NTT DoCoMo—Japan's leading mobile provider. His company would become the first to launch a global 3G network.

"Just as we did not foresee the development of e-mail, the World Wide Web or other popular services when the PC was first introduced, we do not know what services will eventually emerge for 3G," said Yrjö Neuvo, executive vice president and chief technology officer at Nokia's mobile phones division in Helsinki. "But we do know that they will come faster" than they did for the PC. In late 2000, articulating the general expectation, Kurt Hellström, Ericsson's CEO, predicted a 3G surge, boldly proclaiming that by 2003, the 3G business would match the size of Ericsson's 2G business.

In this brave new world of 3G, everyone would win. Telecom operators would be able to charge a premium for the extra service, which would make up for declining voice traffic revenues, and handset makers could sell everyone new phones that supported the technology. Customers were thrilled by the prospect of the portable Web, and analysts praised companies for embracing a bold new (and profitable) future. Governments were excited by the prospect of auctioning off spectrum rights—the permission operators would need to transmit their signals—to the highest bidders. And content partners like ESPN, CNN, and the BBC were enthusiastic about the prospect of new revenue streams enabled by delivering information to consumers anytime, anywhere. In a 2000 article, even the historically austere *Economist* embraced the excitement and expectations for "the intoxicating combination of two of the fastest-growing technologies of all time: the mobile telephone (perhaps a billion subscribers worldwide by 2003) and the Internet (more than 400 million predicted users by 2003). Put those together . . . and you have the justifications for 3G fervor."

In the rush to bid for 3G licenses in Europe, telecom operators spent more than $125 billion in government-run auctions for spectrum rights. They then spent an estimated additional $175 billion to build out their networks, one-by-one updating the radio towers all across Europe to work on a 3G network. The excitement was palpable, and the expectations were huge.

Armed with this knowledge, Nokia entered the fray to deliver the first 3G handset to the European market. It believed its competition with Ericsson was a classic race for first-mover advantage: that operators and customers would embrace the first quality device to market. But focused as they were on executing better than their competition, they were blindsided by co-innovation risk. As Nokia, and the entire sector, would learn: this was just a race to the starting line. They would need to wait there for years before co-innovators were ready and the real race to profits could begin. Had they used a wider lens, they would have done things differently.

Building a 3G Phone

Nokia had been working on 3G prototypes since the early 1990s, when the early protocols for 3G were being established in Europe. But even with deep expertise in the handset market, the challenges kept growing. It was hard enough to build a 2G phone that could smoothly handle bouncing radio signals from one base station to another, stay powered all day, and fit into a user's pocket. Delivering a functioning 3G phone entailed heroic innovation efforts on the part of handset makers and their entire supply chain. As one observer noted, "The 3G handsets, on which Europe has wagered much of its tech future, are by far the most complex consumer electronics devices ever designed. To succeed, they must combine the wealth of applications available on a computer with the roving versatility of a mobile phone. The trick is to wedge all of this into a sleek little machine equipped with multiple radio bands and days and days of battery life—and it must sell at an affordable price."

It was a huge execution challenge, but in the end, Nokia did it. When the company launched the 6650 phone in 2002, it became the world's first GSM/WCDMA-compliant (compatible with networks throughout Europe and Asia) 3G firm. The celebration was intense. They had delivered the product. They had beaten Ericsson. They were first!

But the euphoric welcome for the 3G handset innovation would prove to be completely out of step with the new world that 3G represented. In 2000, Nokia had forecast that by 2002 more than 300 million handsets would be connected to the mobile Internet. The actual number was closer to 3 million (with the vast majority on Japan's NTT closed DoCoMo network, using DoCoMo—not Nokia—phones). The 300 million target was eventually reached, but not until 2008—a six-year delay that set back not just market adoption but, even more painful, revenues, profits, and growth.

At the root of Nokia's mistake was a fundamental misunderstanding of co-innovation risk. The company did not fully appreciate just how dependent the success of its magnificent handset was on the successful commercialization of other innovations yet to be developed by a host of unfamiliar partners. The 3G vision was not one of new and better handsets. It was a vision of an entire mobile lifestyle—personalized videos streamed to your phone, location-based services, automated payment systems, applications to empower a mobile workforce—that was enabled by new and better handsets. And unless and until these other partners delivered on their innovations, Nokia's 3G handset would create about as much new value as a $400 paperweight.

Assessing Risk

Nokia was a brilliant, innovative company at the height of its powers in the 1990s. And yet it fell into what, in retrospect, seems like an obvious trap. It won its race but missed its goal. How could they get it so wrong? It was not because they underinvested. It was not because executives were undermotivated. And it was not because managers lacked competence. It was because they focused all their energy on executing their own projects and commitments. This is of course admirable, but when these commitments depend on other developments for their success, "simply" executing on your job is not enough.

A lot of things have to be managed, and managed well, for a project to succeed. In assessing execution risk—the magnitude of the challenge associated with completing the project on time and to spec—leaders often have to manage not only their own teams but also an array of other suppliers who provide critical inputs to the project. For example, delivering a 3G handset would require Nokia to develop radically new algorithms for signal processing, new circuit designs for power management, new interface designs, etc., all of which it was capable of doing on its own. But it would also require Nokia's suppliers to develop new chipsets, more robust memories, batteries . . . the list goes on.

Project managers obsess over specifications and deadlines, finding ways to close the gap between where they are today and where they need to be by a certain date. Aligning, motivating, and cajoling the right people to get on the right team with the right resources is the hallmark of execution. Nokia succeeded in all of these areas, and the company's ability to deliver its 3G handset was impressive.

Driving the transition from 1G to 2G handsets required just this sort of heroic effort from handset makers. And achieving differentiation in the heyday of 2G was similarly a matter of innovative design integrating innovative components. Here, successfully managing execution risk—delivering better, sleeker handsets with longer battery life and better screens—translated into project success. As soon as a great handset was launched, it was embraced by mobile operators who then passed it on to end users. In the 2G world, the winning formula was both familiar and clear: deliver the right project, on time, to spec, ahead of your rival.

The transition to 3G, however, was of a qualitatively different nature. With 3G, a handset's value creation depended not just on its own quality but also on the quality and availability of a broad variety of complementary products and services that were key enablers of the vision of mobile data. Here, managing execution risk is necessary, but far from sufficient, to ensure project success. The critical consideration for a handset maker in a 3G world is not just whether it can successfully innovate and deliver a 3G phone,

Figure 2.2. Elements of execution risk for a 2G mobile handset.

but whether and when actors *other than handset makers* are going to successfully deliver their own innovations to make the 3G mobile data service vision a reality.

Consider what it means to offer a service like customized streaming video that delivers live clips of the customer's favorite sporting events. This is exactly the sort of value-added subscription-based service that was expected to attract users in droves to the 3G network. Of course you need a smartphone. But what else?

You need video conversion software to reformat television images to fit different sized mobile phone screens. Who makes that? Not Nokia.

You need database and router innovations that will allow operators like France Telecom and Vodafone to know which customers signed up for which streams, on which payment plans. Who makes that? Not Nokia.

You need a digital rights management (DRM) solution to assure content owners like ESPN and Disney that their precious intellectual property will not be pirated in the ether. Who makes that? Not Nokia.

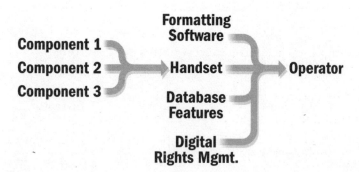

Figure 2.3: Execution risk and co-innovation risk for a 3G handset in the real-time streaming video case.

Collaboration = Dependence

When your ability to successfully commercialize your innovation depends on your partners' ability to successfully commercialize their own innovations, your approach to assessing and managing risk must change. The extent of your co-innovation risk depends on the joint probability that each of your partners will be able to satisfy their innovation commitments within a specific time frame. How should you assess the probability of success?

Most organizations have an established routine for conducting due diligence—consulting with their managers, double-checking with their suppliers, examining their historical precedents—to develop a confidence level about the likelihood of an initiative's successful completion (to spec, on time). In ecosystem settings, you must undertake this same level of due diligence with all co-innovators. But it is the way you integrate your separate find-ings that will shift your perspective.

Imagine yourself at a meeting with three partners to discuss the attractiveness of a potential collaboration. All of you commit to assigning your organization's best resources to your respective initiatives, and all believe that the likelihood of delivering your part of the solution within one year is very high—85 percent. Assume that these individual estimates are accurate. How confi-dent should you be in the success of this joint venture?

The logic of co-innovation is a logic of multiplication, not aver-ages. The nature of joint probability is that the true likelihood of an event taking place equals the product (not the average) of the underlying probabilities. For example, if I flip a coin, I have a 50 percent chance that it will land on heads. If I flip it four times, I still have a fifty percent chance that it will land on heads in each independent instance, but I have only a 6.25 percent chance that

it will land on heads all four times (.5 x .5 x .5 x .5). The same
rules apply in co-innovation. While each supplier has a better
than eight-in-ten chance of succeeding independently, the chance
that they will all jointly succeed at the end of the year is the product
of their independent probabilities. In this case, it is 0.85 x 0.85 x
0.85 x 0.85, or 52 percent.

Fifty-two percent. Imagine your typical project review meetings—
where everyone is confident in his ability to get the job done. How
common is it for confident managers to recognize the frailty of
their joint effort?

Now suppose that one of these partners is responsible for a

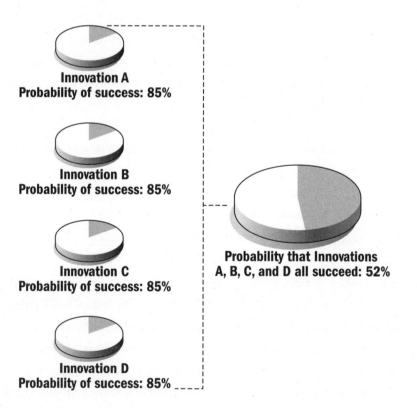

Figure 2.4: The difference between independent and joint probabilities.

particularly challenging development effort and that his probability of success is 20 percent? With just one weak link among the four, the joint probability tumbles to 0.85 x 0.85 x 0.85 x 0.2, or 12 percent.

Twelve percent—let that sink in (but don't let it sink you). Is 12 percent a bad number? No. There is no such thing as a bad number. There are only bad expectations. Twelve percent is fine, as long as you understand the true probability of success and make your choices based on this knowledge. If the loss is affordable, and there is learning to be had, then maybe it's a worthwhile bet. If the potential payoff is twenty to one, then a 12 percent bet can be very attractive indeed. There is no problem with making a 12 percent bet, as long as you know it's a 12 percent bet. The key is to understand the true probability in advance and make sure that, with full knowledge of the risks, you still want to take the bet.

Problems arise when we gloss over co-innovation risk, when we fall into the trap of averages, believing that "since my own initiative has a high chance of succeeding, and since my other three partners are confident too, the total venture is pretty secure." *The trouble begins when we make a 12 percent bet but think that the odds are 85 percent.*

Managing Co-innovation Risk

For investors, identifying co-innovation risk is the key to making smarter bets. For managers, identifying co-innovation risk opens up new avenues for action. Beyond the go/no-go decision, recognizing co-innovation risk can also affect the way in which you develop your strategy and manage your initiative. What are some risk-mitigating actions you can take if you see that one or more partners may diminish your chance of success?

One clear option is to add resources—money, talent, or both—
to bolster development effort. But whose efforts should you support? Deploying resources to reinforce a weak link in the chain
can have a much greater impact on your success than reinforcing
your own innovation. A 10 percent increase in your own odds
(from 85 percent to 95 percent) may reduce team anxiety, but it
moves the joint probability by only 2 percent (from 12 percent to
14 percent). In contrast, increasing your weakest partner's odds by
10 percent (from 20 percent to 30 percent) changes the joint probability by 6 percent (from 12 percent to 18 percent). The number
may look low, but it's one and a half times more likely to succeed
than the initial configuration, and also substantially more likely
to succeed than if you focused your efforts in-house. With the
joint probabilities becoming clear, it may even make sense to take
resources *away* from your project to bolster the overall effort: if
reallocating resources can improve your partner's odds (from 20
percent to 30 percent) proportionally more than it decreases your
own odds (say, from 85 percent to 75 percent), then you will be
increasing the chances of success to 16 percent.

Alternatively, you could consider deploying resources to entice
multiple parties to work on the same challenge: if we have two
partners, each with independent 20 percent odds, working on the
same problem, the expected probability of solving the challenge
doubles. The chance of success is now 24 percent.

Another option is to reevaluate the vision in order to deliver,
at least initially, a more modest value proposition. If your weak
link has a probability of success of 20 percent, your total probability is brought down to 12 percent. If you divest yourself of this
link altogether—for example, giving up on the notion of customized streaming video content and, instead, settling for noncus-
tomized video channels, which would eliminate the need for the

database innovation—then you eliminate its impact on your odds. The probability rises to 61 percent. There is a clear trade-off here: a higher chance of succeeding with a more limited value proposition. But, in some cases, it's better to accept a smaller win than to risk losing the game entirely. Whether this is the right choice in a given situation will depend on how well your organization can accept risk and how much is at stake with a particular innovation.

Finally, recall that these probabilities do not characterize whether a development effort will ever succeed. With more time and resources, odds increase. Rather, these probabilities characterize whether an effort will succeed in a given time frame. As such, a final lever to manipulate is expectations regarding timing. Opting for a less aggressive timeline may go against the grain, but it gives your slower co-innovators the chance to catch up.

An important note: these numerical values illustrate the argument. In real life, of course, we don't have access to such precise probabilities. We can, however, use simple assessments of risk—a one-to-five scale or high/medium/low risk across the system— and apply the same logic. In settings where risk levels are more difficult or costly to specify, going through this exercise will help identify which risk components would be of greatest value to explore in depth.

The key is not the numbers. These are here to clarify the intuition of what it means to manage in a world of dependence and joint probabilities. The key is to identify co-innovation risk and its potential effects. With a narrow focus on execution risk, these effects and these choices are hard to see and therefore hard to manage. When we use a wider lens to identify co-innovation risks more clearly, our approach to many strategic choices—scope, timing, partnering, leadership—changes dramatically.

Nokia Then and Now

Nokia won the race for the 3G phone, but it was the wrong race. In late 2002, Nokia was first to market with the release of the 6650 in Europe, and in North America soon after. It was a hollow prize. The real race could not begin until the digital services were available. The 6650 was a Ferrari in a world without roads. In the absence of critical complements, the 3G offer was but a shadow of its promised self—a souped-up 2G service rather than the radical shift into a brave new world of mobile digital data service that impelled billions of dollars in investment.

It wasn't until the late 2000s that the vision of mobile digital services for the mass market finally began to materialize, most notably with the emergence of Apple's iPhone in 2007. Through 2010, Nokia was the world's biggest producer of 3G phones. But, as the "smart" in smartphone shifted from the handset hardware to software apps running on the phone, Nokia seemed unprepared. The phones were fine as products but impoverished as solutions. The very essence of the game had changed under their feet.

In his "Burning Platform" memo, outlining the dire straits facing Nokia, newly appointed CEO Steve Elop acknowledged that "the battle of devices has now become a war of ecosystems, where ecosystems include not only the hardware and software of the device, but developers, applications, ecommerce, advertising, search, social applications, location-based services, unified communications and many other things." It is a battle in which success means attracting and retaining, beyond customers, co-innovators. In February 2011, in acknowledgment of its changed circumstances, Nokia allied with Microsoft, signing on to the latter's Windows Phone operating system, pulling the plug on the Symbian platform it had nurtured since 1998. The future came, but it came late, and Nokia was not prepared for its implications.

Asking Not If, but When

Nokia's 3G misadventures with co-innovation risk are far from unique. Philips Electronics' misadventures with HDTV in the 1980s ended in failure not because the company couldn't deliver a great television with superior picture quality—it did so beautifully. The problem was the late arrival of high-definition television cameras and transmission standards, which left Philips with a $2.5 billion write-down that shook the financial stability of the company to its core. Philips was right about the vision but wrong about the timing: HDTV was the wave of the future, but the wave didn't arrive on the mass-market shore until the late 2000s. Unfortunately, being half right provides little comfort in the midst of overall failure. This same story is being repeated today in the saga of three-dimensional television as leading firms like Sony, LG, and Toshiba have made huge investments in a race to the start line, where they wait restlessly for the arrival of 3-D programming—which may or may not come—to unlock the market's potential.

Too often, managers ask the wrong question when they begin their innovation journeys. In meetings and boardrooms, over lunches and drinks, the talk is focused on "Can we do it?" and "How can it be done?" Whether the vision is customized pharmaceuticals, solar energy generation, an innovative design for a drill bit, or a new line of organic-based shampoos, with enough talent, money, and time, most goals can be achieved. Like Nokia, ambitious companies will time and again set their sights on the next exciting innovation. And, like Nokia's, success will too often prove ephemeral. Why?

The real question, is not *if* it can be done, but *when*. Not just *when* will we be able to complete the project, but *when* will we be able to align the necessary ecosystem for the complete value proposition to become a reality. The question of *if* speaks to success in the abstract. The question of *when* speaks to returns, to attractiveness, to viability in the concrete. Being right about the vision offers cold comfort if we are wrong about the timing. Bad timing expectations are a core source of innovation failure. But as we will see in chapter 6, understanding the nature of co-innovation can offer powerful clues for setting better timing expectations.

The Good News

Confronting the real odds of success can be jarring. But if we can see the risks clearly—removing them from our blind spot and placing them squarely in our focus—then we can manage them. Not knowing the real odds does not make the risk go away; it simply leads us to set unrealistic goals at the beginning and to suffer the cost of failure at the end.

Co-innovation risk doesn't make things bad—just different. Once we understand co-innovation risk, the ways in which we prioritize opportunities and threats, the ways we think about market timing and positioning, and the ways we think about designing our offers and mitigating our risks all shift. Indeed, the very ways in which we measure and reward success all change. This is the good news: by seeing what is actually driving the odds of success, we improve our odds of success.

CHAPTER 3

Adoption Chain Risk:

Seeing All the Customers Before Your End Consumer

A range of intermediaries stand between you and your end customer: the distributor who needs to agree to bring your product to market, the retailer who needs to agree to showcase it, and the salesperson who needs to agree to sell it. Your success depends on each of these partners adopting your innovation and seeing the value it will create for them. If any one of these partners is not on board, you will never be able to reach your end customer. When does the best product lose? When the consumer doesn't have a chance to choose it.

In this chapter we will examine *Adoption Chain Risk*, the extent to which partners will need to adopt your innovation before end consumers have a chance to assess the full value proposition. Here our question shifts from whether partners can deliver the required co-innovations to whether they will see the value proposition as beneficial not only to the end consumer but to themselves as well.

We all know that a natural tension exists between those selling a product and their target buyers. At its root is a misunderstanding over the notion of value—the balance between costs and benefits. Although both innovators and consumers use the terms "cost" and "benefit" to describe the way they think about value, they think about these terms in very different ways.

Consider Microsoft's Office 2007 suite. When launched, the vast majority of enterprise users agreed that Office 2007 was superior to its predecessor, Office 2003. It had better code quality, was more reliable, and offered more features. According to Jeff Raikes, president of the Microsoft Business Division, "The 2007 Microsoft Office system RTM [release to manufacturing] completes the most significant improvements to the products in more than a decade." And the price difference was zero: enterprise customers pay Microsoft a fixed fee, per user, per month, to lease their Office software, independent of which version they use. Firms would need to pay just as much to use Office 2007 as Office 2003. A better product for the same price, this looks like an obvious win. But decision makers at most companies large and small chose to stick with the clearly inferior Office 2003. Why?

(Total) Cost vs. (Relative) Benefit

Innovators and customers view "benefits" and "costs" from very different perspectives. Missing the difference is a recipe for disaster.

Innovators think about benefits in terms of what their product actually provides—the absolute benefit delivered to the customer. But customers think about benefits in terms of added value—the relative benefit delivered by the product compared to the available alternatives. Each group also has a different understanding of costs: while innovators tend to think of the price they will charge for their innovation as the determinant of customer cost, customers conceive of cost in terms of that price *plus* all the other changes they need to undertake in order to use the innovation (beyond the initial outlay, the cost of retraining, equipment upgrades, etc.). While innovators tend to focus on delivering an offer whose absolute benefits exceed the purchase price, adoption happens only if the customer sees a clear surplus: that is, the *relative* benefits must exceed the *total* cost. These differences can lead to an assessment gap. And this gap can lead to disappointment.

Office 2007 adoption lagged because, even if the price was free, the total cost was high—too high for most customers to justify. If

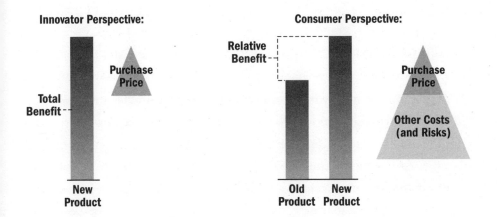

Figure 3.1: Innovators and consumers have different views on what constitutes "benefits" and "costs."

you are a CIO considering an Office upgrade, your notion of cost goes well beyond price to include retraining, hardware upgrades, changeover time, and all the unknowns that inevitably come with making a company-wide change. While the sales rep brags that Office 2007 is 99.9 percent compatible with 2003, what keeps the customer up at night is that last 0.1 percent. Not knowing whether the incompatibility affects the ninth iteration of Helvetica font or the critical invoicing macro changes the attractiveness of the offer dramatically (perceived risk is an important contributor to non-price cost). And even though none of these costs show up in the innovator's revenues, they are all charged against the innovation's benefits. Frustratingly for Microsoft, Office 2007's total costs exceeded its relative benefits for most customers.

In the end, the key driver of adoption for Office 2007 wasn't a change in its relative benefit, but rather a reduction in its total cost that accrued over time. As noncompatibility issues and bugs were gradually resolved, and as companies followed the natural replacement cycles for computer hardware, it became easier to justify the 2007 upgrade . . . until the next version of Office was launched in 2010, and the entire cycle started anew.

Superabrasive Grinding Wheels

Take a look around your home. It's likely that you have abrasives to thank for the smooth shape of your sink's faucet, the sharp edge of your cutlery, and the tiny components that run your computer. Abrasives are the category of hard materials used to shape and polish softer objects in a variety of manufacturing processes. They constitute a mature industrial market with revenues of close to $4 billion in 2010.

Figure 3.2: A grinding wheel in use. *(Photo compliments of Saint-Gobain Abrasives.)*

Superabrasive grinding wheels were an innovation born when GE introduced synthetic diamonds in 1955. At the time, industry leaders agreed that superabrasives were going to transform the industry. They were much harder than their conventional brethren (aluminum oxide, silicon carbide) and therefore offered many benefits: they were more durable, required less frequent dressing (the process by which the outer layer of the wheel maintains its coarseness and its trueness), could be used at higher speeds, allowed higher production rates, and could enable better products with finer finishes and tighter tolerances. Superabrasives were more expensive, with prices up to thirty times more than those of conventional wheels; but they lasted up to a hundred times longer. With their longer lives, their higher production rates, and their decreased need for human intervention, superabrasives would offer greater overall efficiency *and* increased performance. Expectations were high.

Despite their grand promise, however, today superabrasives make up only approximately 15 percent of the abrasives market. This innovation has had nearly fifty years to make good on initial excitement and capture market share, yet it has reached a plateau. What went wrong?

The relative benefit of superabrasive grinding wheels was real and high. But the total costs were high as well. They were not just more expensive to buy; they imposed new costs in their use. To take advantage of higher grinding speeds, manufacturers would need to invest in higher-speed grinders (the powered machine tools used for grinding). The greater hardness of the wheel meant that the machines used to dress them needed to change too. And because higher speeds required greater precision in the way in which the wheels were dressed and balanced, it meant staff needed to be retrained and upskilled.

The balance of total cost/relative benefit depended on the application. Where tight tolerance requirements combine with long production runs, such as selected manufacturing steps within the aerospace and automotive sectors, total surplus was positive, and superabrasive grinding wheels made deep market inroads. But outside these niches, taking into consideration the total cost of the value proposition, most of the market opted to stay with traditional grinding wheels.

At 15 percent market share, were superabrasive grinding wheels a successful innovation? It depends on your viewpoint. Success is always assessed relative to expectations. For early enthusiasts, superabrasives' niche market is a disappointment. After all, what promised to be a revolution ended up being a small but healthy advancement in the industry. However, a number of firms developed a balanced view of the relative benefits and total cost of superabrasive wheels. They designed their organizations, and allocated their resources, with the niche market as an explicit target. For them, 15 percent market penetration is a high-margin cause for celebration.

From Adoption to Adoption Chains

Many innovations rely on a chain of intermediaries that stand between them and their end customer. Consider your breakfast choices. Before you get to decide whether you like the new Strawberry Delight Cheeriflakes that the marketing folks at Z Cereals are trying to sell you, many other actors need to get on board. The plant manager needs to decide when and how to adjust production to accommodate the new recipe; the distributor needs to agree to accommodate a more complex product range; the salespeople need to promote it; the grocer needs to agree to allocate shelf space to the new offer (which means taking away space from others); and everyone needs to converge on prices and terms. Together they comprise the Cheeriflakes adoption chain. And if any one of them decides against supporting the new offer, consumers will never have the chance to make the purchase. And company Z will never have the chance to make the sale.

Once products are established, these handoffs are seamless (indeed, achieving this seamlessness is a primary element of what it means to be established). But new offers can disturb the existing routines. When adoption chains are fragile, outcomes are uncertain.

In today's interdependent world, the successful innovator must treat each partner as a customer even if they are not in a direct business relationship.

Whereas the logic of co-innovation is one of multiplication (not averages), adoption chains follow a logic of minimums (not net surplus). Consider the two innovation proposals, A and B, illustrated in figure 3.3. Both require that your innovation pass through two intermediaries before reaching the end customer: the distributor who sells the product to a retailer, who then sells the product to the end customer. Innovation A creates high value for the innovator (it is highly profitable, with surplus of +4), high value for the distributor (high margins and low handling costs, with surplus of +3), slightly negative value for the retailer (higher up-front costs, retraining and after-sales service headaches, despite slightly higher margins, with a deficit of –1), and very high value for the end customer (surplus of +5). Innovation B creates positive, but low, surplus for everyone in the chain (surplus of +1 for each of the four actors). The net system surplus created by innovation A is 11 (4 + 3 – 1 + 5). The net system surplus created by innovation B is 4 (1 + 1 + 1 + 1). Which one should you bet on?

We have all been trained to "focus on the customer," to "listen to the voice of the customer," to try our utmost to "delight the customer." But as the adoption chain makes explicit, we rarely have just one customer. Which customer in the chain is most important? All of them! Each and every intermediary that is part of the ecosystem needs to see surplus from adopting the innovation. A single instance of rejection is enough to break the entire chain.

The logic of adoption chains dictates that innovation A, despite the far higher value it creates for the end customer (+5 vs. +1), and the higher net surplus that it creates for the chain as a whole (+11 vs. +4), will fail. It will fail, not because the end customer won't prefer it, but because the end customer will never have the chance to choose it. As long as the retailer is worse off with innovation A than with its current alternative, it will be a broken link in the adoption chain. Ironically, despite its lower value creation, innovation B will sail through the adoption chain. A moderate, but

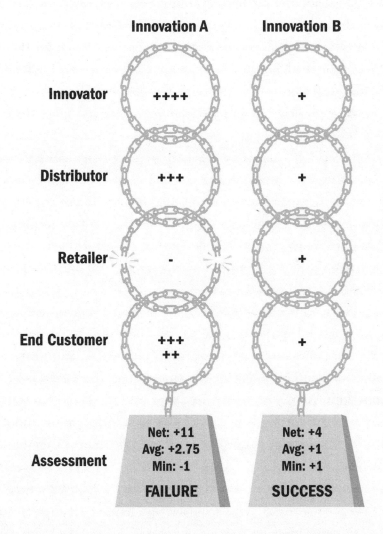

Figure 3.3: Surplus along the adoption chain for two innovations. Expect failure if any link is negative.

attainable, win is infinitely more valuable than a huge, but hypo-thetical, victory.

As was the case with co-innovation risk, however, the very act of recognizing the sources of adoption chain risk can suggest ave-nues for addressing it. Rather than abandon the effort, the wise innovator will revisit the plan for innovation A with an eye to elim-inating the retailer's deficit—by finding an alternative partner, an alternative path, or by reallocating surplus along the chain to put the retailer in positive surplus (for example, shifting the end con-sumer's surplus from +5 to +3 to move the retailer from –1 to +1). These mitigation steps are themselves innovations to the struc-ture of ecosystems. *Risk can be managed proactively, but only if it is recognized in advance.*

As clear as this may seem in theory, in practice it's easy for inno-vators to overlook the incentives and motivations of the intermedi-aries to which they have no direct links. For this reason, it can be tempting to turn your gaze inward to issues you can better con-trol. But ignoring your dependency on others will not prevent them from upending your innovation efforts.

The key is to ask the difficult questions *from day one*, unearthing what everyone in the adoption chain needs in order to push your innovation down the line. What are these difficult questions? They are the questions that probe for constraints and problems rather than for support and uncommitted agreement. Recall Michelin's run-flat disaster from chapter 1. What if the company had asked the garages not, "Will you be willing to incorporate new machinery and retrain your staff to fix PAX tires?" but rather, "Will you be willing to incorporate new machinery and retrain your staff to fix PAX tires *even before there are a substantial number of PAX tires on the road*?" The answer would have been unpalatable. But it would have been critically useful. Michelin's leadership would have had the opportunity to modify their strategy to figure out how to manage the garage adoption problem in advance of the PAX launch, instead of scrambling and improvising when it was already too late.

If the innovators at Michelin had truly understood the nature of their adoption chain challenges, then they might have approached the market in a very different way. For example, one option (among others) could have been a multiyear exclusivity to a single carmaker. This would increase the carmaker's differentiation advantage compared with its their rivals in exchange for a strong guarantee that their dealerships would all install repair equipment in their service garages within the first year of launch. With the equipment installed, these dealerships could service PAX tires on any make of car, such that when exclusivity ended, a service infrastructure would be in place. In chapter 8 we will explore such strategies under the heading of establishing a minimum viable footprint. For innovators who believe they have a great product, as Michelin did with PAX, proactively limiting the size of early success can be a challenging strategy to embrace. But the disaster of launching without having addressed adoption chain problems is far worse. The only way such an option can be debated seriously is if you begin your discussion with a wide-lens view of your ecosystem.

Adoption chain risk is a product of the tug-of-war between innovation and the status quo. The challenge is convincing critical partners that there is positive value for themselves in joining your efforts when they feel they are doing just fine as is. Sometimes this is a matter of communication. But as we will see in the following example, often it requires innovating the innovation ecosystem itself.

How Digital Cinema Turned a Minus into a Plus

In the late 1990s, Hollywood's dream factory had a dream. Since its earliest days, stars—from Charlie Chaplin to Cary Grant to Marilyn Monroe to Julia Roberts to Russell Crowe—were all projected into our imaginations through the same technology: celluloid film. Digital technology was enabling new magic in almost every stage of moviemaking (special effects, editing, sound), but movie projection remained the province of the industry's standard for over half a century. While the click-clack sound of spinning reels may evoke nostalgic smiles among audiences, for the studios the need to print, ship, and retrieve bulky canisters of analog film was both costly and inefficient. And in the midst of a fertile technology boom, a new way to distribute, project, and enjoy movies finally emerged in the form of digital cinema.

As analog formats throughout the media world were falling away, the transition to digital cinema seemed a certainty. Building on the foundations already laid by the development of the laser disc and, more successfully, the DVD, the technology path to digital was clear. The value proposition was unambiguous: higher-resolution picture quality, better protection from piracy, flexibility of programming, the potential for 3-D screening, and—for the studios—the elimination of costly film prints. Bringing this exciting new technology to the masses required technological advances. Most crucial was the development of the digital projectors themselves. Happily for the studios, the first commercial DLP (Digital Light Processing) projectors became commercially available as early as 1996.

However, as we saw in the case of 3G in chapter 2, the mere availability of an innovation is not enough for success: often, a multitude of co-innovation challenges need to be overcome in order for the value proposition to become a reality. The co-innovations required for digital cinema's progress included analog-to-digital film conversion and data transfer/storage capabilities. These were ready too. The 1989 development of the digital telecine scanner, which rapidly converts film into a digital format, meant movies could be shot on film yet projected digitally. This was a great boon to the studios because it allowed them to avoid the challenge of convincing directors and production staff to adopt new equipment and techniques. Storage and delivery capabilities also fell in line: hard drives at the time were capable of storing digital films if they were split over several drives, and content could be efficiently distributed over the Internet through the newly developed high-speed T3 lines. By 1999, these key elements of the digital cinema projection system were ready, and moviegoers were treated to digital cinema for the first time when *Star Wars: Episode I—Phantom Menace* was screened in Los Angeles and New York.

In February 1999, the *New York Times* heralded "Digital Projectors Could Bring Drastic Changes to Movie Industry." But unfortunately for the studios, despite the viability and availability of this miraculous system, and its potential to save them millions in costs and add millions in revenues, digital cinema would spend the next seven years in limbo. Yet, while digital projectors were used in less than 5 percent of U.S. cinema screens by the end of 2006, they were used in nearly 40 percent by the end of 2010. Why did it take nearly a decade for this appealing new technology to reach more than a handful of cinephiles? And what happened to finally speed its ascent? The answer lies in the adoption chain.

Who Stands to Gain?

In the digital cinema ecosystem, there were several key players who had to adopt the technology in order for it to reach the general moviegoer.

The big movie studios certainly saw value in supporting and advancing digital cinema. After all, leaving celluloid behind also meant avoiding the $1 billion spent annually on the printing and shipping costs associated with traditional film. The cost of producing one film print falls between $2,000 and $3,000 per print. So, if a typical U.S. nationwide release is shown on about 3,000 screens, the studio's printing cost alone can come to $7.5 million.

Digital cinema also opened up the possibility of releasing the film in what insiders call a "day-and-date" approach. Traditionally, movies were rolled out in a staggered fashion, which allowed the studios to control and minimize the costs of moving expensive, heavy prints around the globe. With digital cinema, films could be released everywhere simultaneously, offering an alternative to pirated films for (over-) eager global audiences. In addition, digital film technology allowed for encryption, which would further help reduce, though not eliminate, film piracy, to which studios attributed a cost of more than $3 billion per year.

The distribution arm of the studios, as well as independent distributors, would also benefit from greater flexibility of tailoring the movie to a specific audience. Going digital meant that subtitles and multiple versions of trailers could be easily adjusted to better target a specific locale. Theater owners could operate more efficiently, with fewer staff required to operate and maintain the projection equipment. Of course, the suppliers of the projectors and equipment upgrades and service technicians for whom digital cinema provided a large new revenue stream saw the obvious value in the digital transition. And moviegoers would be winners too, enjoying an enhanced theater experience. Better resolution meant the images were brighter, crisper, and more engaging. "What do you think people notice the first time they see film and digital cinema projected side by side?" asked Jim Korris, the executive director of the Entertainment Technology Center at the University of

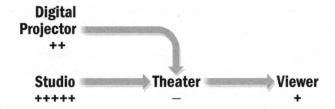

Figure 3.4: The digital cinema ecosystem in 2003.

Southern California. "It's that people realize they've been looking at films that flicker their entire lives. Digital cinema is like looking out of a window. It's rock steady."

So if everyone saw the benefit of adopting digital cinema, where was the problem? The answer lies with one player for whom the benefits were high, but not high enough to offset their total cost: the movie theaters. Imagine that it is 2003 and you are the owner of either an independent movie house or chain of theaters and have been following the development of this new technology. Digital cinema is an exciting possibility: you could easily adjust which movies would be shown on which screen and thus take advantage of demand spikes for surprise hits; you've heard it would be possible to stream live sporting events and concerts, offering a new way to entice audiences; and there is even talk of mainstreaming 3-D movies, with higher ticket prices, but which could be screened only with digital projectors. The relative benefit is high.

But so is the total cost. Cinemas are relatively low-margin businesses. Historically, they make most of their profits not from ticket sales but from concessions. For the vast majority, the $70,000–$100,000 per screen conversion cost necessary to buy the digital projector and supporting hardware and software for an upgraded projection room was prohibitive. Moreover, digital projectors have a life span of only ten years, compared to thirty to forty years for traditional projectors. Add a lack of clarity about competing format standards that would take years to get settled, and it is easy to understand why a theater owner considering the ongoing maintenance costs of this new, uncertain technology, and weighing it against the familiar celluloid alternative, would hold off incorporating digital cinema. "Maybe we'll do it next year . . . or the year after that."

Director James Cameron, long a proponent of the promise of going digital, noted, "Digital cinema and 3-D open the door for filmmakers to mine completely new creative territory. It's up to exhibitors, now, to adopt these new technologies on the display side, so that audiences have a reason to seek out the cinema and leave their computer and flat-screen TVs." Easy for a director to say—for him, the relative benefits far exceeded the costs. Exhibitors saw it differently. "We can't afford to put in expensive equipment," said Ayron Pickerill, a small theater owner in Montana. "And if we don't have it, and everything is digital, we'll be out of business; that's all there is to it." Is it any wonder their preferred tactic was to delay?

In the early years of the new millennium, this attitude was the consensus among theater owners across the country, causing a crucial rupture in the adoption chain. Unless the costs and risks of adoption for cinema owners were lowered, mass audiences were unlikely to ever enjoy the experience—and studios the cost savings—of digital cinema.

Technology Standards Are Not Enough

In 2002, seven major motion picture studios—Disney, Fox, Metro-Goldwyn-Mayer (MGM), Paramount Pictures, Sony Pictures Entertainment, Universal Studios, and Warner Bros. Studios—came together to form Digital Cinema Initiatives, DCI. "We thought that if we left it up to the exhibitor it would never happen," noted one Warner Bros. executive, Dan Fellman. The group's purpose was to establish a set of specifications for digital cinema with the hope that industry-wide standards would reduce uncertainty and encourage adoption. The struggle took years of tests and trials. Julian Levin, DCI chairman and executive vice president of digital cinema at 20th Century Fox, put it mildly when he observed that the work was "taking a little longer than people had expected." In July 2005, DCI published its specifications, finally resolving the issue of standards.

But even with these technology standards in place, theater owners were unwilling to take the digital cinema plunge. Another innovation would have to be introduced into the ecosystem in order to equalize adoption risk. Interestingly, in this technology-driven transition, the missing piece of the puzzle wasn't a technical advancement but a financial one.

How an Innovative Financial Framework Saved Digital Cinema

Digital cinema promised big net benefits not just to the movie studios but to the aggregate ecosystem as well. The problem, however, was that the benefits weren't distributed evenly. And because theaters were a critical link in the chain—meaning that there was no way to do without them or go around them—it would be impossible for digital cinema to succeed as a win-win-lose-win solution. The challenge was to find a win-win-win-win proposition—some way to share enough surplus with theaters to make them *want to* come on board.

With a clear recognition of digital cinema's advantage to their bottom line, studio heads fought to get a solution in place before confidence in digital cinema's potential began to fade. With the press calling the digital cinema arena "the Wild West," and exhibitors far from a sure bet for digital adoption, something needed to happen. As National Association of Theater Owners president John Fithian put it: "They'll either have their act together this year, or it'll fall apart."

The Virtual Print Fee Solution

In an industry in which the links between parties were nonexclusive (each studio would send the same movie to many theaters; each theater would screen movies from many studios), what was needed was an elegant way to enable studios to contribute to the theaters' digital conversion cost in a way that all the parties regarded as fair.

Across the sector, the idea of a financing model in which the studios would contribute to the cost of converting to digital was being raised. The studios agreed: "The proportion of financing should be relatively proportional to the benefits enjoyed by each party," said Chuck Goldwater, CEO of DCI. The National Association of Theater Owners voiced its concern that whatever form the financing plan took, it must be industry-wide, "supported by all major motion picture studios through one financial entity or a consortium of financial entities, and that all other motion picture studios willing to participate in the plan must be given the opportunity to do so." This would avoid the nightmare of fragmentation, where different studios had divergent financial requirements and terms for screening their films. The challenge was not just of agreeing to subsidize the theater owner's participation, but of finding the right way to bring them on board (and doing so without running afoul of antitrust concerns).

Enter VPF. The VPF (virtual print fee) program is a financing innovation that allows studios to subsidize the high cost of digital cinema adoption in theaters. It does so by introducing a new actor into the ecosystem—the digital theater integrator. Under the VPF model, instead of theaters being forced to cover the costs of equipment upgrades and maintenance, this new third-party integrator pays the initial outlay for the equipment and assists with technology integration and maintenance. The integrator's profits come from a five- to ten-year lease-to-own arrangement with the theaters, which is subsidized by the VPF. For every movie that is projected in digital rather than analog form (thereby saving the studio thousands of dollars in avoided printing, shipping, and retrieving costs), the studio shares the benefit by paying a virtual print fee of approximately $1,000 to the digital integrator on behalf of the exhibitor. Over the life of the contract, the VPF arrangement can cover approximately 80 percent of the exhibitor's conversion costs. At the end of the contract, the exhibitor retains the equipment, ensuring that digital cinema becomes industry standard.

The VPF breakthrough emerged in 2005, ultimately allowing

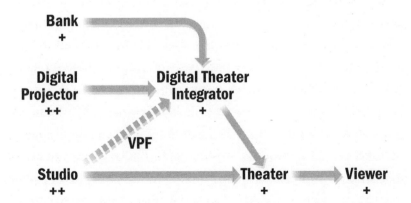

Figure 3.5: Digital cinema ecosystem after the introduction of the virtual print fee (VPF).

the digital cinema dream to become a reality. The year 2006 is widely considered to be the transition year for digital cinema, as theaters across the country began to gradually embrace digital cinema's promise. And in 2007, theater chains AMC Entertainment, Cinemark USA, and Regal Entertainment Group—who collectively controlled almost 30 percent of the total screens in the United States—formed their own integrator organization, Digital Cinema Implementation Partners (DCIP), further spurring the mass adoption of digital cinema.

In 2009, James Cameron's 3-D record-breaking sci-fi megahit *Avatar* led moviegoers to realize that modern three-dimensional offerings were a far cry from the gimmicks of the 1950s. In the first two months after *Avatar*'s release, 81 percent of its $601 million U.S. box-office gross came from 3-D ticket sales. Riding high on the public's enthusiasm for 3-D, Disney's *Toy Story 3* became 2010's top-grossing picture. By the end of the year, 38 percent of U.S. screens and nearly 25 percent of global screens had converted to digital. The revolution had finally arrived.

Digital cinema still faces hurdles. As new generations of equipment emerge, there will likely be issues of quality control and compatibility as everyone along the adoption chain gets up to speed. Additionally, the question of long-term digital storage is problematic. The costs of digital preservation are significantly higher than for traditional film. And there are questions about the sustainability and size of ticket premiums for 3-D movies. Despite these concerns, the shift to digital cinema will be nearly impossible to reverse. As the installed base of analog projectors shrinks, as analog manufacturers abandon the market, and as studios stop printing and shipping analog film, we can expect celluloid film to go the way of the LP record album in the age of digital music and become a niche curiosity.

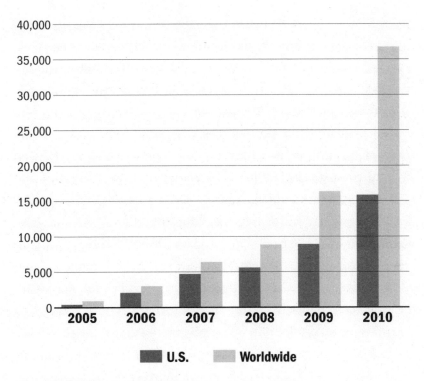

Figure 3.6: Digital cinema installations.

Evaluating the Success of Digital Cinema

At first glance, the progression of digital cinema can be viewed as frustratingly slow. After all, in the near ten-year lag before widespread adoption, everybody could have been enjoying its benefits. But, if we look at the path to full adoption, we see that the incremental steps taken—and the order in which they were taken—were necessary for digital cinema's ultimate victory. The studios were smart to set industry standards first, preventing the possibility of high-tech chaos as different players supported divergent technologies, hindering the consensus necessary for a mass rollout. Three-dimensional content was ramping up, creating visible consumer demand for digital cinema that theater owners could see. But, offered a financing solution and VPF payments, exhibitors didn't need to wait for 3-D hits before agreeing to take their initial steps. Digital-enabled theaters began to enjoy added revenue from new sources of content such as live broadcasts of sporting events, concerts, and opera. And having taken the initial steps, upgrading to support the slew of digital and 3-D offerings that soon arrived was more a hop than a leap. And as the benefits to theaters of adopting digital cinema have grown, studios have been able to reduce the VPF subsidy for later adopters.

We will explore the confluence of leadership and successful innovation in depth in chapter 5. But it is worth noting here that in order for mass adoption of digital cinema to take place, leadership was required from the only party with enough economic incentive and resources to matter: the movie studios. Neither the independent distributors nor the equipment suppliers were in a position to lead due to fragmentation, limited bargaining power over exhibitors, and a lack of financial sway. The integrators made a great leap for digital cinema by launching the VPF model, but without the participation of the studios, the financing framework would have fallen flat. It was the studios that, by initially moving away from celluloid film, setting digital standards, and later collaborating with digital theater integrators, cleared the path for the widespread adoption of digital cinema. With VPF, the studios stepped into a new role, creating a new set of links into the ecosystem. They found a brilliant solution to induce the digital changeover. And by limiting their participation to a fixed time window, they also engineered a process to get themselves back out of the way, and off the hook, once the system is entrenched.

Targeting Adoption Chain Solutions

Adoption chain problems require adoption chain solutions. Not just intervention and investment, but intervention and investment targeted at the right place in the right way. The movie studios could have spent their resources trying to create excitement with audiences, producing more movies, or pushing more advanced technologies, but none of these would have affected the core problem that held back digital cinema. Instead, by identifying the theater operators as the key bottleneck, they knew where to focus their efforts, creating a financing solution targeted specifically at turning exhibitors' negative assessment to a positive one.

For superabrasive grinding wheels, understanding the total-cost/relative-benefit balance has meant adjusting market expectations. Recognizing that the advantages offered by this superb innovation were accompanied by a host of nonprice costs, the industry understood that the net proposition would be positive for only a subset of users, and it found ways to run profitable operations targeting the niche rather than the mainstream.

Seeing the realities of your adoption chain risk puts you in a better position to make smarter choices early on. Wise innovators will have a plan for addressing every adoption chain link with negative surplus *in advance* of their launch. They will modify their strategy to create surplus for the problematic adopter or find a way to reach their end customer without the help of the problematic link. And if they cannot find a way to address these challenges, they will understand that they may well be better off foregoing the opportunity and shifting resources to the next option on their list.

A wide-lens perspective will help you uncover the true nature of adoption chain challenges. With a clearer view, the outlines of the right solution will be easier to see. Developing them may require effort and innovation, as was the case with VPF, but the returns from these efforts are high. You must not avert your gaze when confronted with a partner with negative surplus. The key is to not rush to action until the fundamental dynamics are clear. It is easy to invest in satisfying end users, but it is not always effective. Remember which customer in the adoption chain is the most important. *All of them.*

■ ■ ■

REFLECTION ON PART I:

INTERNAL AND EXTERNAL ECOSYSTEMS
ALL AROUND YOU

The majority of the examples in this book unfold in the "external ecosystem," among the different organizations that need to come together for a new value proposition to succeed. But all the ideas we will examine also apply to the "internal ecosystem" that is your organization. Whenever a new initiative depends on the support of other parts of your organization to succeed, you face a combination of co-innovation and adoption chain challenges. Will the finance department need to change the rules for allocating costs and revenues across product divisions to encourage cooperation? Will the service organization be able to support the solution after it is launched? Will the incentive scheme make the innovation attractive for the sales force to embrace or do they need new incentives? Legal, Human Resources, Marketing . . . once you identify what current relationships within the organization need to change to allow your initiative to succeed, you can start strategizing about how to manage the dependencies. The logics we have explored, and the tools we are about to develop, hold independently of where you draw the boundaries of the firm. While the role of power and politics is different inside and outside your organization, the wide-lens principles are the same.

Similarly, while the examples are often drawn from product and technology settings, the ecosystem ideas and principles apply equally in service and nontechnology settings: human resource executives trying to push through a new talent management system; school superintendents overseeing curriculum reforms; government officials assessing the merits of different policy and regulatory choices; community organizers developing a plan for bettering neighborhoods. While they differ in the resources they can utilize and the goals they are trying to achieve, they can all benefit from a comprehensive set of tools for seeing and managing interdependence to increase their effectiveness and odds of success.

Finally, although the arguments are developed in the context of introducing new innovations, they speak directly to the globalization challenge of entering new geographic markets. Here, the message is clear: beyond adapting the value proposition to suit local preferences, it is essential to be aware of how the change in locale affects the ecosystem context into which the adapted value proposition is deployed. Using the lenses of co-innovation risk and adoption chain risk, alongside the tools to come, can help surface hidden differences across markets that will impact how you prioritize deployment and how you reshape the localized offer itself.

In some ways, ecosystem challenges can be viewed simply as traditional project management challenges writ large. The major difference, however, is the way in which you draw the boundaries around the project. A narrow lens will leave you focused on execution risk, prone to ignore the implications of co-innovators and adoption chain partners. But as we will see in the upcoming chapters, assessing your innovation through a wide lens will not only change what you see, it will also change how you approach key strategic choices (part 2) and reveal new ways to fundamentally change the nature of the game (part 3).

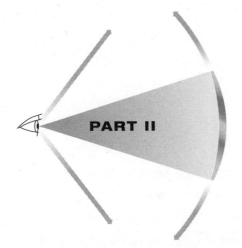

PART II

Choosing Your Position

III. Winning the Game

II. Choosing Your Position

I. Seeing the Ecosystem

Chapter 6
Right Place,
Right Time

Chapter 5
Roles and
Relationships

Chapter 4
Mapping the
Ecosystem

Main Cases:

E-Books and Inhalable Insulin	Electronic Health Records	Music Players and Semiconductor Lithography

Tools:

Value Blueprint	Leadership Prism	First-Mover Matrix

Mapping the Ecosystem:

Identifying Pieces and Places

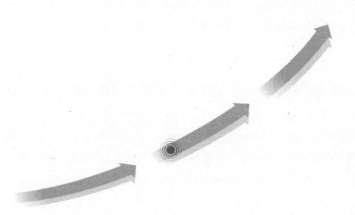

I magine four partners at a conference table discussing their companies' latest groundbreaking endeavor. Even when they share a vision of what they are trying to accomplish—what new value their joint initiative is trying to create—they will often have different visions of how their separate efforts come together. Who will move first? Who is dependent on whom? Who faces the customer and who is just an invisible cog? In a world of supply chains, the linear path of A hands off to B hands off to C hands off to D is relatively clear. A world of ecosystems, however, is a world of permutations—A, B, C, and D all need to work together simultaneously, and the combinations of possible roles is vastly greater. The challenge is usually not that partners openly disagree about what must happen first or who is responsible for what; it's that these questions are not sufficiently explored. Instead, having agreed on the end vision, the partners assume that they also agree on the best path to get there. A dangerous assumption indeed.

When strategies explicitly call for collaboration, they make an implicit assumption about structure. In this chapter we will make this assumption explicit by exploring a systematic approach to clarifying not just who needs to come together to bring your value proposition to life, but also where they will be positioned and what risks lie within the plan. By making the structure of the ecosystem explicit, we will make our strategies more robust.

From Value Propositions to Value Blueprints

Your value proposition is a promise. It is a vision of the new value that your innovation efforts will create, as well as who this value will be created for. For effective, efficient innovation, you need a way to translate the value proposition into action. When the value proposition requires multiple elements to converge, you need an approach that will allow you to assess alternative configurations and generate shared understanding and agreement among the partners as to how these elements should come together.

To do this, we will use a mapping tool I call the *Value Blueprint* (see figure 4.1). The value blueprint is related to value chains and supply chains. The main difference is that while the latter tend to focus on the linear sequence of handoffs from suppliers to producers to distributors to end customers, the value blueprint is explicit about the *specific* location and links of complementors that lie off the direct path to market but are nonetheless critical for success. Indeed, it is the ease with which these off-path partners can be overlooked using traditional strategy tools that gives rise to the innovation blind spot. The value blueprint sits at the heart of all the tools we will develop from here onward.

The value blueprint is a map that makes your ecosystem and your dependencies explicit. It lays out the arrangement of the elements that are required to deliver the value proposition—how the activities are positioned, how they are linked, and which actor is responsible for what. We begin by identifying the full set of partners and specifying their positions; the suppliers your project relies on, the intermediaries that lie between you and your end customers, and the complementors whose offers are bundled at different points along the path. We then identify the changes in the activities and links that we are expecting from each participant. Finally, we assess how these changes affect the likelihood that the entire system will actually come together to deliver the value proposition.

We have already looked at value blueprints when describing many of the cases so far—Michelin's PAX System, 3G telephony, digital cinema—to identify the actors and the links that make up the ecosystem.

The steps to construct a value blueprint are straightforward:

1. Identify your end customer. Ask: *Who is the final target of the value proposition? Who ultimately needs to adopt our innovation for us to claim success?*

2. Identify your own project. Ask: *What is it that we need to deliver?*

3. Identify your suppliers. Ask: *What inputs will we need to build our offer?*

4. Identify your intermediaries. Ask: *Who stands between us and the end customer? Who touches our innovation after us, and to whom do they pass it on the way to the end customer?*

5. Identify your complementors. For each intermediary ask: *Does anything else need to happen before this intermediary can adopt the offer and move it forward to the end customer?*

6. Identify the risks in the ecosystem. For every element on the map ask:

   a. *What is the level of co-innovation risk this element presents— how able are they to undertake the required activity?*

   b. *What is the level of adoption risk this element presents—how willing are they to undertake the required activity?*

      It is often most productive to characterize the status of each element of your innovation effort along a green–yellow–red traffic light continuum. For co-innovation risk, green means that they are ready and in place; yellow means that they are not yet in place, but that there is a plan—they may be late, but they'll get there; and red means that they are not in place, and there is no clear plan. For adoption risk, green means your partners are eager to participate and see clear surplus from their involvement; yellow means they are neutral but open to inducement; and red means they have clear reasons to prefer the status quo and prefer not to participate in the proposition as it stands. In assessing the risk implied by new links, it is important to consider the incentives of each linked party to choose to interact in this new way.

7. For every partner whose status is *not* green, work to understand the cause of the problem and identify a viable solution.

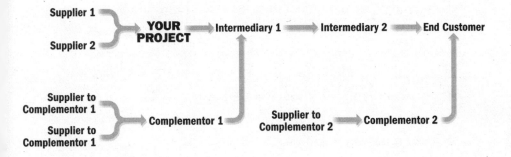

Figure 4.1: A generic value blueprint maps the actors and the links that make up the ecosystem.

8. Update the blueprint on a regular basis. Your value blueprint is a live document, and as conditions change over time, it will need to be modified accordingly.

By making these relationships clear, the value blueprint forces everyone involved in the conversation to confront the challenges that lie beyond their own immediate responsibilities; to consider how they want to organize and address the risks that are inherent in every collaborative endeavor; and to deal with these issues proactively. Note that what matters here are the elements, not their ownership. When different elements come from the same firm, they must be still be assessed separately.

It is rare for a significant innovation to start life with an all-green-light blueprint. It is also not necessary. Some yellow lights are acceptable, as long as they are accompanied with a plan to turn them green. Yellow lights are sign of delays to come, but they need not be showstoppers. Red lights, however, are a major problem. Any red light that appears on your map—whether

because of a partner's inability to deliver or unwillingness to cooperate, or due to a problem on your part—must be addressed. This
can mean any number of scenarios, from managing incentives to
finding a way to eliminate the troublesome link in your blueprint.
Often, identifying the most promising path is an iterative process.
Only once you have made the necessary adjustments can you confidently start your engines.

This is not to say that seeing all green guarantees success; you
will still face all the usual unknowns of the market and its vagaries. Execution is critical. But unless you have a plan to get to
green across the board, expect delays and disappointment even if
you deliver your own part flawlessly.

The Elusive E-Reader

Let's apply the value blueprint methodology to examine why Amazon and Sony achieved radically different outcomes in developing
the market for e-readers, and how these outcomes were rooted
in the starkly different approach they used to construct their ecosystems.

Even before the World Wide Web, technology companies had
been trying to figure out how to make books digital. As early as
1990, Sony introduced its Data Discman Reader. But with limited
content (a small number of reference titles, novels, and the Yellow
Pages), which was only available on Sony-published CDs, few consumers found the $550 device attractive. The Rocket, developed
by NuvoMedia in 1998, was the first product to allow e-books to
be downloaded from a PC. That same year the SoftBook, developed by SoftBook Press, arrived with an internal modem that
made the PC unnecessary, and in 2000, Gemstar released two
models that boasted backlit screens and long battery life. Each

Figure 4.2: An early attempt at an e-book reader—Sony's Data Discman (1990). *(Alan Levenson / TIME & LIFE Images / Getty Images.)*

of these innovations furthered e-reader technology but was beset by limitations: they were too expensive, too clunky, and their eyestrain-inducing screens made reading on them a pain (literally). Simply put: they didn't offer a better experience than a good old-fashioned paperback, and so customers saw no incentive to purchase them.

Then, in 2000, in what many industry insiders viewed as proof that the electronic book was ready for the mainstream, online retailers sold 500,000 downloaded copies of Stephen King's novella *Bag of Bones* in a mere forty-eight hours. All the big publishers—Random House, HarperCollins, Simon & Schuster, TimeWarner, and Penguin—launched digital imprints, hoping to take advantage of this new way to attract readers, and the following years saw growth in the e-book sector. Random House's e-book revenues doubled; Simon & Schuster saw double-digit growth in e-book sales; Microsoft and Acrobat competed to distribute software to support the new e-books. Yet no electronic reading device gained traction in the market, and e-books remained an R&D curiosity. As Carolyn Reidy, the president of Simon & Schuster, pointed out: "The hardware was not consumer-friendly and it was difficult to find, buy and read e-books." Mass adoption by consumers remained elusive.

It was into this environment that Japanese electronics giant Sony launched its PRS-500 Portable Reader in September 2006. This new effort came two years after the failure of its Librié e-book in the Japanese market. There, the Librié was undone by the inertia of the Japanese publishers. Paltry content and intense digital rights management (DRM) that deactivated e-books after only a few months in order to reduce piracy sealed its fate. Sony had high hopes that the U.S. market would be more receptive to the value offered by its device. CEO Sir Howard Stringer noted, "We've been very cautious in launching [the Reader] because, as you know, it failed in Japan two years ago. This is a totally different version with totally different economics and software."

Retailing at $350, the Reader was almost 20 percent cheaper than the Librié. It also boasted a brighter screen, longer battery life, and more memory. Users could choose from approximately 10,000 titles available at Connect.com, the online bookstore that Sony launched alongside the Reader. E-books could be downloaded (in Sony's proprietary BBeB format) onto a PC and then transferred from the PC to the Reader via USB cable.

Sony's Reader was a Lamborghini to the Model Ts of earlier attempts. Slim and lightweight, with a highly praised "electronic ink" technology that was as easy on the eyes as was paper, it was touted as the iPod of the book industry. It achieved what no other reader had managed: a reading experience that approximated traditional print, with all the advantages (storage, search, and portability) inherent to digital media. The launch met with much fanfare from the press, where the Reader was hailed as "the electronic gadget that could change the way we read."

So why, having delivered this exceptional device, did Sony fail to deliver on its promise? The answer lies in its value blueprint.

Finding Clues in Blueprints

Sony's target customer was clear: mainstream book readers.

Its project (the Reader), its suppliers, and its intermediaries (the retailers that would sell the hardware) were clear as well.

Sony brought massive technology resources to the Reader project. It developed both the Reader hardware as well as a new DRM standard (BBeB) for managing content. It successfully partnered with cutting-edge suppliers like E Ink, the company that developed the remarkable screen technology. It leveraged its brand, marketing prowess, and existing distribution relationships to ensure getting the Reader into customers' hands. At launch time, Sony had green lights across the line of the project, supplier, and intermediaries.

But a great e-reader is not enough to complete the value proposition for the customer. They also need something to read. Enter Sony's complementors.

Sony's plan for getting e-books to readers depended on bringing on board authors, publishers, and its own e-book retailer, Connect.com.

Even though some authors could have been convinced to issue

e-books (yellow light), it was the publisher who controlled the flow of content. And publishers were problematic on both the co-innovation and the adoption fronts.

As co-innovators, publishers looked like reasonable partners. They would need to innovate, modifying their internal processes and systems to manage and package e-books. This was a technical hurdle but a manageable one. *Publisher yellow light.*

As adopters, however, publishers were highly ambivalent about whether and how to approach e-books. First, the economic and legal aspects of this new offering had to be hashed out: What is an e-book worth? What will the royalty payouts to authors be? How should the contractual language read? What would margins look like? The publishers—conservative firms clinging to a traditional business model—would not commit to e-books until these concerns were settled. And Sony was in no position to settle them. *Publisher red light number one.*

Second, was the question of standards. Various e-book file formats were vying to establish themselves with publishers and hardware firms. They ranged from proprietary formats from giants like Adobe and Microsoft, to efforts by focused start-ups, to open-source proposals. But the very idea of having their copyrighted content in the digital wilderness—a hacker's dream—sent shudders down the publishers' spines. Competing digital rights management (DRM) systems were making diverse claims and pushing different methods to protect this precious content, but the cacophony of approaches added to the confusion, lowering publisher confidence in committing to any one approach. Sony's proposed DRM solution, the BBeB format, was thus just one more unproven option in a crowded field. *Publisher red light number two.*

Turning any one of these lights green would not be enough. Sony would need a clear path to turn *all* of them green before publishers would come on board in a meaningful way.

E-book distribution was a separate problem. Sony launched its own online retail outlet—Connect.com—to establish a retail foothold on the content side. But establishing an online store, and attracting both suppliers and buyers to make it a worthwhile venue in which to transact, is a very different challenge than creating a great piece of hardware. So even though Sony had a plan, it was far from clear that it would work. *Yellow light; maybe red.*

Throw in uncertainty about demand and you have room for a lot of debate, a lot of confusion, and a lot of hype but not a lot of progress. The Reader was a great device, but customers weren't flocking to buy it. Combine this with a decade-long history of false starts, and where was the incentive for publishers to commit to Sony's specific e-book vision? The traditionally risk-averse industry preferred to debate standards while taking a gradual, wait-and-see approach to digitizing their books. They much preferred the status quo of selling hard-copy books through their established online and brick-and-mortar retailers.

And as long as publishers held back, end consumers would be held back too. A lack of adequate content meant Sony's Reader wouldn't make a dent in the marketplace; slow sales of the device dissuaded publishers from swiftly resolving the myriad issues that would result in more content. At the time of the Reader's launch, Nick Bogaty, executive director of the International Digital Publishing Forum (IDPF), noted: "I've always said that four factors need to be in place for the market to take off. You need a device that makes reading pleasurable, content at the right price, a great selection of content, and e-books that are easy to use."

Sony got the first element right. But even at 10,000 titles, the available content on its online store was a haphazard collection—by way of comparison, a well-stocked independent bookstore carries upward of 50,000 titles, while the average Barnes & Noble superstore carries as many as 200,000 titles. Moreover, the price

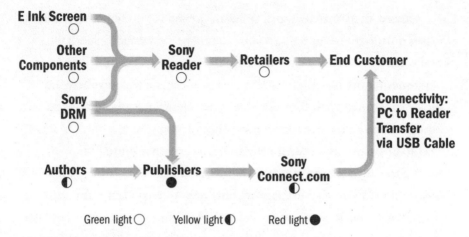

Figure 4.3: The Sony Reader value blueprint at launch.

points for the e-books that were available were not low enough to convince readers to invest the initial $350 for the device. Although backlist titles went for as low as $4, the difference between the price of a best seller on Connect.com and the same hardcover discounted by conventional booksellers was negligible.

Further reducing the benefit to users was the multistep process required for them to acquire an e-book. With a book already in mind, you would still have to search for an online bookseller, find the book on its Web site, purchase the title from an unfamiliar vendor, download the file to your PC, and then hook up your Reader for the transfer. For the bulk of consumers, it was easier to head to the local bookstore or order a hard copy online than to deal with a spotty inventory, an arbitrary backlist, an inconvenient process for getting e-books onto the Reader, and high prices. Sony's advances in e-reader devices, while significant, were meaningless if the printed book remained the better experience.

As this chaos played out for electronic books, Sony sat on its golden egg and waited. And waited, and waited. . . . In the excitement of launching the PRS-500, it was clear that Sony was focused on delivering great hardware as the key to unlocking the potential of e-books. But while the hardware was certainly a cornerstone, it was not the whole structure. As the value blueprint shows so starkly, a plethora of dependencies had to be managed for e-books to gain traction.

Had Sony's management attempted to create a value blueprint during the early stages of its Reader development, they would have been forced to confront the fact that they had no clarity for how content was going to make its way onto the device, no matter the excellence of the hardware. The exercise would have forced a change in their path: find a way to eliminate the publisher's red lights, reduce expectation for the launch, or drop the Reader and pursue another project.

The fact that the Reader was a green light for Sony did not offset the red lights elsewhere. And, without a clear plan for how to turn red to green, the Reader was dead in the water. As an e-book reader, Sony's device was commendable; as an e-book solution, it was a flailing effort.

Sony's journey in e-readers is a story of a great product waiting for a market to arrive. Unfortunately for Sony, when the market did finally emerge, it did so on Amazon's terms.

The Kindle Conquers

As the publishing industry haggled over how to make e-books a winning proposition, Amazon entered the fray. In 2007, the largest book retailer in the world launched the Kindle, the innovation that finally brought e-books into the mainstream. As a device, the Kindle was regarded as inferior to Sony's Reader. Described by

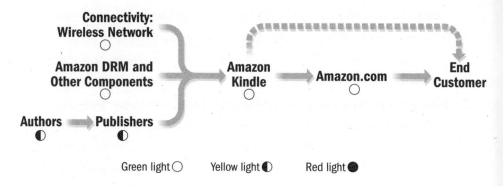

Figure 4.4: Amazon's Kindle value blueprint at launch.

one analyst as "downright industrially ugly," it was larger than the Reader, weighed more, and had an inferior screen. Moreover, it was a *very* closed platform that was able to load content only from Amazon, and which precluded users from transferring the books they purchased to or from any other device, sharing with friends, or even connecting to a printer.

How could Amazon engineer a triumph with a weaker product? The company did it by engineering a solution. Take a look at Amazon's value blueprint above. What is the primary difference between the approaches taken by Sony and Amazon?

For readers, the Kindle provided a one-stop shop, a simple, inexpensive way to purchase and enjoy anything from *Jane Eyre* to the latest *New York Times* best seller. Presenting the Kindle, CEO Jeff Bezos announced, "This isn't a device, it's a service." Unlike Sony's Reader, the Kindle offered a complete experience for the customer: an expansive library of books, initially including more than 90,000 titles and growing to approximately 330,000 within two years; the right price (while a new hardcover usually costs around $25, most Kindle books, including new titles and best sellers, were $9.99 or less); and the ability to download the book instantly using Amazon's wireless network. Bezos explained his vision for a streamlined user experience: "You shop right from the device. . . . One of the reasons people are so excited about this device is because it doesn't involve the PC. They don't have that dread of 'how am I going to get this to interoperate with my PC?' It just works as a stand-alone device."

It is easy to praise the value proposition. But, as evidenced by the initial excitement around the Reader, Sony had a compelling vision too. The key difference was the way in which Amazon aligned the ecosystem to bring its value proposition to life. Often overlooked, but critical to its success, is what Amazon changed on the back end to create its offer. As its value blueprint makes clear, in order to create this seamless experience, Amazon changed the way critical elements of the ecosystem were configured by both extending its successful position in retailing *and* simplifying the value proposition for all the other parties involved. A few yellow lights, yes, but a clear plan for turning them all green.

As one of the Internet's biggest success stories, Amazon's powerful retail platform gave it enough leverage to approach publishers with several innovations that would encourage the creation of digital books for Kindle. After all, this "King of the Retail Jungle" was responsible for approximately 30 percent of books sold in the United States. Publishers had to pay attention. But Amazon *did not* simply bully publishers into supporting the Kindle. Amazon created conditions in the ecosystem that made joining the long-awaited e-book revolution a more attractive proposition for publishers than any previous attempt.

First, Amazon tackled the DRM issue. The Kindle was both closed and proprietary, meaning users could not print their e-books, read them on another device, or share them with other people.

While this restriction was a turnoff for consumers, it was critical to reducing publishers' perceptions of risk and total cost in making their adoption decision. In the language of chapter 3, shifting readers from +4 to +2 is well worth the effort if it will shift the publishers from −1 to +1. In looking at the total ecosystem, Amazon made the wise choice to reallocate value to its weakest link, the publisher. This strong DRM system gave publishers a much-needed sense of security at a time when the dangers of piracy—as exhibited by the popularity of file-sharing sites within the music and movie industries—topped the list of their digital concerns.

Amazon also increased the relative benefit for publishers by effectively subsidizing their participation through a counterintuitive retail model. Traditionally, bookstores pay publishers a certain percentage of a book's list price to acquire a title and then sell it to their customers for a profit. (So, if the list price of a book is $25.00, and the publisher charges the bookstore 50 percent, the bookstore pays only $12.50. If the store then sells the book at 20 percent off the list price for $20.00, it makes $7.50.) For e-books, Amazon paid the publisher 50 percent of the list price of the print version but then sold the e-book for $9.99. So, if the price of a standard hardcover at the time was $25.00, and Amazon paid the publisher $12.50, the company actually lost $2.51 on each e-book sold. To jump-start the e-book ecosystem, Amazon sacrificed some e-book profits up-front, but it was able to make up much of the difference in its sale of the $399 Kindle device (which, by some estimates, earned margins of $200 per unit).*

In the short term, everybody was a winner: the publisher received the same amount it would have earned from a print version and

---

* In 2010, at the behest of publishers, Amazon abandoned the fixed retail price model, allowing publishers to set e-book prices directly and receiving a 30 percent commission on each sale.

saw a boost in sales; the customer enjoyed a cheaper, and some would say better, reading experience without sacrificing breadth of book choice; and Amazon emerged as the leader in the electronic book revolution. It was a position worth fighting for. According to Forrester Research, by 2015, U.S. consumers are expected to spend $3 billion on e-books. This forecasted growth is especially impressive given that, according to the IDPF, sales of e-books in 2007 were only around $10 million. But the Kindle's entrance into the market lit a fire: by the end of 2010, e-book sales were fast approaching $120 million. By the time Amazon launched the Kindle 3 in 2010, it held 80 percent market share of electronic books and, with estimated sales of the Kindle at 6 million for that year, 48 percent market share of e-readers.

Deconstructing E-Book Value Blueprints

Sony and Amazon built their value blueprints using identical pieces but placed them in very different positions. In contrast to Sony, Amazon followed a blueprint that put it firmly in the role of integrator, bringing together all the various elements required for value creation itself, and delivering a comprehensive, intuitive experience to its customers. It took on far more responsibility for organizing the system than did Sony. While Sony assumed its red lights would somehow work themselves out, Amazon turned red to green by taking the lead and blazing a trail for the entire industry.

Amazon's and Sony's efforts to conquer e-books were the inverse of one another: Sony enjoyed competence in its hardware but was a stranger to the ecosystem; Amazon was well positioned in the ecosystem but was less competent with its hardware. The e-book ecosystem—like so many of today's innovative efforts—is ultimately a system of interdependencies. Success would not be determined on the basis of a winning effort at any single point; it required moving the entire cohort of partners in the same direction. We will further explore strategies for successful ecosystem construction and expansion in chapters 7 and 8.

Sony's hyperfocus on the hardware element left an enormous blind spot that ultimately undid its efforts. Its pioneering Reader may have been first to market in 2006, but by 2010, it was fighting to hold the number five spot in the e-reader marketplace.

In contrast, Amazon's willingness to enter the fray with a plan to drive the entire system forward meant that e-books could finally gain traction, and do so on Amazon's own terms.

The e-book market continues to evolve with the entry of new platforms, like Apple's iPad and Barnes & Noble's Nook, as well as with the unbundling of reading platforms from reading hardware, like the Kindle app. The competitive dynamics are sure to change as the ecosystem matures.

The one certainty throughout will be that, in the race between competing blueprints, the winners are the ones who have a plan to get to green across the board. Drawing a value blueprint is an exercise in discipline that forces you to construct the entire picture around your project *at the beginning*. It shows you where you have a coherent strategy, where you have inconsistencies, and where you are just hand waving ("Oh, that will eventually fall into place"). And because it gives you a clear view of all the elements and their status, the value blueprint allows you to manage your red and yellow lights from the get-go, rather than as a series of tactical adjustments in the face of go-to-market surprises.

To see why up-front clarity is so important, consider one of the most disappointing flops in the history of the pharmaceutical industry: inhalable insulin. See if you can find the point of breakdown—the blind spot moment.

The Promise of Inhalable Insulin

At the turn of the twenty-first century, pulmonary insulin was a darling of the pharmaceutical industry's biggest players, and for good reason. There are more than 347 million diabetics world-wide. Of the 25 million diabetics in the United States, 4.8 million have to administer their own insulin, the vast majority of which do so by needle injection (a tiny fraction use insulin pumps). By allowing patients to use an inhaler (similar to those used by asthma patients), pulmonary insulin administers the correct dose of insulin noninvasively—without a dreaded needle. It was an innovation that could reduce pain, add convenience, and enhance the quality of life of millions of diabetics around the world.

The excitement around pulmonary insulin was enormous. "We've never had such a response to anything we've done," stated Dr. Jay S. Skyler, associate director of the Diabetes Research Institute at the University of Miami Miller School of Medicine and a lead investigator on a patient study. The popular press embraced the idea, with headlines like *USA Today*'s "Insulin Without Injections Nearly a Reality," and the London *Times*', "The Potential for Inhalable Drugs to Change Medicine Is Breathtaking."

It's easy to see why the world was excited. Besides patients' understandable desire to escape the needle, inhaled insulin prom-ised greater compliance. More than 90 percent of diabetes patients suffer from type 2 diabetes, the onset of which is often due to poor lifestyle choices. Diabetes has a high level of deniability in its ini-tial stages. The stigma associated with the disease, and the dis-comfort of daily insulin injections, means that there is often a five- to eight-year window between the time patients need insulin and the time they actually begin treatment. This new, noninvasive option would help patients accept their illness earlier, saving lives and societal costs through the avoidance of later-stage complications. (The estimated total annual costs of diabetes in the United States alone is over $200 billion.) A 2003 report from Pharmaprojects articulated these expectations: "These products, if approved, could expand the market for insulin to several times its current value as a result of patients being more willing to take the therapy if it is offered via inhalation rather than by injection."

In 1998, the race to market for pulmonary insulin began in earnest. Novo Nordisk started development of AERx. Later that year, Pfizer and Aventis entered a joint venture to create Exubera. Eli Lilly entered the development race with a device dubbed Air. And in 2001, MannKind Corporation, a California biotechnology start-up, joined in with its own pulmonary insulin effort.

As clinical trials and market research were painstakingly conducted, enthusiasm grew and everyone in the sector was predicting a blockbuster win. In 2001, Morgan Stanley Dean Witter forecasted Exubera annual sales of more than $1.5 billion by 2009; three years later, Credit Suisse First Boston predicted the device would garner $1 billion annually by 2007.

Expectations were high, but developing inhalable insulin was a monumental task. Peter Brandt, Pfizer's U.S. head of pharmaceutical business, stated the challenge: "Pfizer had to create the means to manufacture inhalable insulin, a substance that had never existed before. . . . Exubera is as much a manufacturing innovation as it is a breakthrough medical advance."

Pfizer led the pack through a combination of its own breakthroughs and its rivals' stumbles. "With a two-and-a-half- to three-year lead time, Pfizer will have a blockbuster product on its hands," predicted Robert Hazlett, an analyst for SunTrust Robinson

Humphrey. And on January 12, 2006, the company announced a business success to match its R&D prowess. Taking advantage of a contractual clause triggered by Aventis's merger with Sanofi, Pfizer successfully sued for the right to buy out Aventis's share in Exubera for $1.3 billion, gaining full control of the drug. This looked like a masterstroke when, fifteen days later, Exubera received regulatory approval in Europe by the EMEA, followed just one day later by approval from the U.S. Food and Drug Administration (FDA).

In its approval, the FDA excluded patients who smoked and patients who suffered from lung degradation or heart disease.

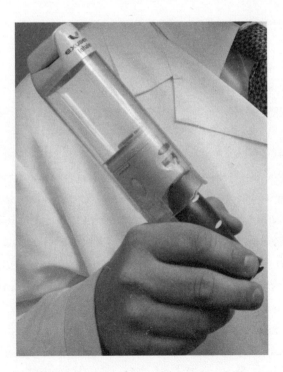

Figure 4.5: Pfizer's Exubera inhaler. *(AP Photo / Mark Lennihan.)*

The FDA also posed a requirement that all patients have a pulmonary function test prior to initiating therapy to make sure their lungs were able to absorb the insulin and recommended a follow-up test six months after initiation and every year thereafter. Neither constraint was regarded as a problem.

Pfizer had won the race, and it had overcome major technological hurdles to do so. The project's risk had been extraordinary—surely an extraordinary win was in order.

Exubera was far from a perfect product, a fact that everyone acknowledged. Indeed, all the pharmaceutical firms developing inhalable insulin solutions, as well as the Wall Street analysts, the broad health-care community, and the press were clear-eyed about a host of limitations. The first-generation inhaler devices were bulky, the powdered insulin was more expensive than the injected alternative, and the novelty of the approach meant that doctors and nurses would need extensive training to be able to teach their patients how to properly use the inhaler.

Still, each of these challenges had been identified years before Exubera's launch, when it was still in early clinical trials. And each of these factors was regarded by Pfizer, the analysts, and the medical community as manageable. Yes, the early devices were regarded as bulky by a subset of patients, but knowing this, Pfizer already had a more elegant second-generation device well under development and had accounted for bulkiness when it set its sales forecasts. Yes, the insulin was more expensive, but this is the case for almost every new drug. Pfizer, no stranger to the vagaries of insurers and formularies, planned for Exubera to graduate to an increasingly favorable copayment tier over time, just as other successful insulin drugs had done in the past. Yes, the device required training, but Pfizer's strategy called for an initial rollout targeting experienced endocrinologists and diabetologists who had "a wealth of experience with not just the use of insulin but the oral agents as well and, most importantly, with this patient population." Its explicit plan was to first get this critical opinion-leading segment on board and only then, four to six months later, start rolling the drug out to general practitioners (GPs) and other nonspecialists who were less expert, more distracted, and generally less open to adopting new insulin therapies.

Pfizer had all these limitations clearly in view and built a strategy that would allow it to overcome them and prosper. At the time of Exubera's launch, Pfizer confidently predicted sales of $2 billion by 2010. Meanwhile, pharmaceutical rivals Eli Lilly, Novo Nordisk, and MannKind were running as hard as they could to get to market and capture some of the spoils. Wall Street analysts saw these limitations as well and incorporated them into their forecasts. These nominally objective critics pushed back against Pfizer's estimates. Both Morgan Stanley and Bear Stearns believed that high manufacturing and education costs would be a problem and estimated $1.5 billion in Exubera sales by 2010. WestLB was even more guarded, projecting "only" $1.3 billion.

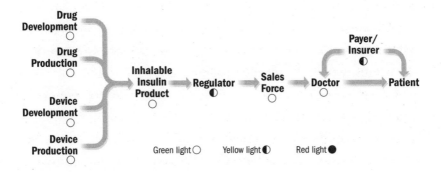

Figure 4.6: Value blueprint characterizing Pfizer's expected path to market for pulmonary insulin in 2005 as the company awaited regulatory approval (excludes pharmacies).

The big debate was whether Exubera would be a *super* block-buster or *just* a blockbuster.

After the FDA approved Exubera for sale in January 2006, Pfizer made big investments in preparing the market: it developed a rich array of educational materials, set up a twenty-four-hour call center for patient support, and trained 2,300 sales reps in the intricacies of teaching and pitching Exubera to doctors and nurses. By October, the company had reached out to more than 5,000 endocrinologists and diabetologists—its target launch group. And in January 2007, Pfizer launched its "full-court press" to GPs and nurses.

Pfizer had a clear view of the challenges—and a clear plan to overcome them. Not a red light in sight.

Or so they thought.

Dead on Arrival

By the end of 2006, Exubera sales were "negligible." Blaming the sluggish initial performance on educational and marketing hurdles, Pfizer looked forward to its full rollout in 2007 with its head held high. The company maintained its projection that sales of Exubera would reach $2 billion, although perhaps not by 2010, as it had previously stated. But by July of 2007, Pfizer reported that sales "continued to be disappointing."

In October of 2007, Pfizer pulled the plug. Exubera was dead. Total sales: $12 million.

Pause for a moment to consider the difference between expectations of $1.2 billion and actual sales of $12 million. That's a miss of one hundred to one. Achieved sales amounted to one one-hundredth of the plan. Staggering. Exubera went down as "one of the most stunning failures in the history of the pharmaceutical industry."

Pfizer's exit was initially regarded as an opportunity by its rivals, whose inhalable insulin offers would address many of Exubera's shortcomings. "The problem is it was kind of like generation zero," said Mads Krogsgaard Thomsen, Novo Nordisk's chief science officer. "All those [unfavorable qualities], the size, the number of steps to administer . . . have been addressed in our product." Lilly president John Lechleiter was similarly confident in his firm's efforts. "[Pfizer's exit] really doesn't diminish our enthusiasm for our product. We believe there's a place for more convenient administration of insulin. As we have said all along, the device, the technology behind the approach that we're taking, we think is going to be more convenient for patients, easier to use. We're not backing away an inch . . . [there is] a big opportunity there for the person that can come along or the company that can come along with the right product."

But within five months, both Novo Nordisk and Lilly would terminate their own inhalable insulin efforts. In the end, Pfizer wrote off $2.8 billion on its Exubera effort. This astronomical figure made Novo Nordisk's $260 million loss on AERx and Eli Lilly's $145 million loss on Air look like relative bargains.

It's tempting to explain away Exubera's failure as rooted in an imperfect product (the bulky inhaler), a burdensome training requirement (every patient would need to be taught, usually by already overworked doctors and nurses), or misestimations of needle phobia and improvements in insulin pens (which undermined the relative benefit of a noninjection-based option). It's also tempting to blame a management team that perhaps fell in love with its own ideas and ignored all these warning signs.

But while these were contributing factors, they cannot explain the failure. Pfizer is a great company, renowned for its marketing prowess. Having worked with thousands of patients and scores of doctors throughout the years of Exubera's clinical trials, having conducted countless focus groups, they knew better than anyone that some patients would embrace the inhaler, while others would balk until a smaller one was available (which is why they were already on their second-generation device). Of course they considered this in setting their expectations. As the world's leading insulin pen producers, Novo Nordisk and Eli Lilly knew more than anyone about improvements in pens and patient reactions to needles but still raced forward with their own inhalable insulin projects. Of course they accounted for the drawbacks of inhaled insulin in their expectations. And as for Pfizer management falling irrationally (or politically) in love with a losing darling, recall that it took a major lawsuit to force Sanofi-Aventis to cede control of Exubera, which they too saw as "the next big thing."

Pfizer, Lilly, and Novo Nordisk were all rushing toward the same goal. This was not a Pfizer miss; this was an industry miss. A failure this big and broad doesn't come from problems with execution or misreading customer preferences. It comes—just like the failures in run-flat tires, HDTV, and 3G telephony—from a blind spot.

The Inhalable Insulin Blind Spot

Every other firm racing to deliver its own inhalable insulin envied the way in which Pfizer overcame the development and manufacturing challenges of both the drug and the device, the way it cleared the regulatory challenge in achieving FDA approval, and the careful (and costly) path it was carving to educate the healthcare community about inhalable insulin. What everyone overlooked, however, was a subtle but critical change in the ecosystem that came about because inhalable insulin . . . *needed to be inhaled.*

When the FDA approved Exubera, it added one crucial caveat by requiring patients to undergo an FEV_1 lung function test, which was performed on a device called a spirometer. The good news was that the FEV_1 was very common and easy to administer—no co-innovation risk here. The bad news was that this made it all too easy to overlook its true implication.

Pfizer's reaction to the news was telling.

Summarizing the market rollout plan for Exubera for Wall Street analysts, the head of Pfizer's U.S. pharmaceutical business explained, "We're starting with the targeting of physicians who are basically large users of insulin now, and therefore have a wealth of experience . . . with this patient population. That therefore, by definition, means you are going to have an awful lot of the endocrinologists in that group. That is, if you will, our first wave of the rollout . . . is to target those highly experienced, primarily endocrinologists, with things like the early experience or starter kits . . ." The plan was to first target endocrinologists and use their buy-in to support the second-wave push to GPs.

At the very same meeting, when asked about how Pfizer planned to respond to the lung function test requirement and the availability of spirometers, Dr. Michael Berelowitz, Pfizer senior vice president in charge of worldwide medical and outcomes research, replied, "As far as the pulmonary function testing required for Exubera is concerned . . . in primary-care practice, there is a requirement that physicians [GPs] be able to do pulmonary function in their patients with asthma and so on. So they have availability of this kind of equipment, and they have comfort with this kind of equipment. That is what we have heard from physicians as we have spoken to them and they become used to the idea. So we don't see that as an issue."

Can you see the contradiction? It went unnoticed before,

during, and after the analyst call—by everyone. But when the plan hit reality, the disconnect was stark.

"We don't see that as an issue." They should have used a wider lense.

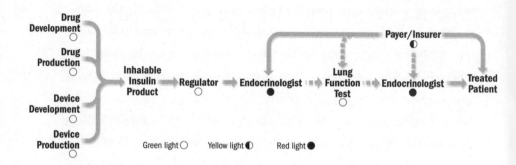

Figure 4.7: Value blueprint of the actual path to market for the first phase rollout to endocrinologists after regulatory approval (excludes pharmacies).

The lung function test would not be an issue for general practitioners. But Pfizer's plan (which followed the tried-and-tested industry norm) hinged on specialists adopting the new product first. There was a critical disconnect between the way the two executives conceived of the plan. A clear value blueprint would have forced the right question to the surface: what does it mean for an endocrinologist to perform a lung function test before prescribing a treatment? Answer: something very different than it would mean for a GP to do the same.

While spirometers are standard equipment in a GP's office, used to test for asthma, they have no natural place in an endocrinology practice. Thus, the specialist would need to refer the patient to another doctor, nurse practitioner, or lab, and then set up a second patient visit before treatment could begin.

Now consider the fact that there is an acute shortage of endocrinologists in the United States. Waiting times for appointments can be three, even nine, months. Indeed, many endocrinologists were so overbooked that they were not taking new patients.

The lung function test requirement means that, beyond assessing the endocrinologist's reaction to the training challenge (which was accounted for), we need to consider how enthusiastic the doctor will be to delay patient treatment for weeks or months—and the patient's reaction to the inconvenience of both the delay as well as the multiple visits. Not to mention the insurer's view on paying for a second specialist visit.

In his postmortem debrief on Exubera in October 2007, Ian Read, Pfizer's then-president of worldwide pharmaceutical operations (and current CEO), commented, "We clearly underestimated the barrier to moving patients or the physician community earlier to Exubera. I think this is one of the major issues we underestimated—the resistance from physicians and patients to going onto Exubera—going onto insulin in any form earlier than they have been to date. So that is one major barrier. The second one is, per se, the burden that the Exubera technology represented to the practice, which went from the lung function testing, the training on the device, and while the size of the device may have been a component of that, I think you have to look at the totality of it."

Had they used a wider lens to look at "the totality of it" from the beginning, Pfizer would have seen the one piece of the puzzle they didn't account for—the blind spot that was so easy to miss unless you were actively looking for breakdowns. This was the log that broke the camel's back.

Like Sony with e-readers, Pfizer succeeded in creating a technology miracle. Lilly and Novo Nordisk were close behind with products that looked even more promising. But what needed improving was not the product; it was the path. Like the significance of the garages in the run-flat case, the lung function test was easy to overlook precisely because it was already available. But there is a crucial difference between being available and being accessible. The moment that the lung function test became a regulatory requirement, success *required* a plan to solve the endocrinologist's "lung-test loop." And in the absence of such a plan, failure was virtually guaranteed.

As of May 2011, the only major firm still working on pulmonary insulin is MannKind, which as of the time of this writing has spent nearly $1 billion of founder Alfred Mann's own money, convinced that the quality of both its insulin and the device is materially superior to those of any of its rivals. (MannKind's MedTone device is one-tenth the size of the bulky Exubera, and its Technosphere Insulin System closely mimics the release of insulin a healthy individual experiences at the beginning of a meal.) Although the FDA denied approval of MannKind's offering in January 2011, according to president and COO Hakan Edstrom, the company is "certainly resolved to pursue" its approval. More than just good luck in developing a great product, I wish MannKind a clear vision in recognizing its ecosystem challenges and finding a way to manage them in advance of launch.

The Value of Value Blueprints

Sony and Pfizer both failed to appreciate the ecosystem structure that their strategies implied. The moral of their stories is that huge allocations of resources and deep wells of talent on their own cannot make up for red lights on the path to success. If your value proposition requires multiple parties to collaborate, building a deep understanding of the structure of collaboration is critical. The fact is, today's complexities require a new up-front conversation that hardworking managers may initially see as over-kill. But gone are the days when "Sure, we'll get to that down the road" will suffice.

Creating a value blueprint is an exercise in team discipline. It forces you and your team to be explicit about your value proposition and about all the steps you'll take to make it a reality. It forces you to see the issues before they become problems. The explicit steps of the exercise require you to ask questions that may otherwise be happily put off or pushed aside, or that you may not even be aware you need to ask. Who exactly is your end customer? The retailer who displays your product? The person who purchases it? The person who uses it? In what order should your partners act? Who passes what to whom? Who is the visible brand and who is the invisible cog? Where do the co-innovators enter the critical path? Who comes first and who comes next? Who is ready and willing? Who is ready but unwilling? Who is neither?

But creating a value blueprint is also an exercise in communication. It forces a dialogue that will bring your assumptions—and those of your colleagues and partners—out of the shadows and into the light. These questions should be asked early. You may be surprised at how often teams working on the same overarching goal have radically different visions of the path. In the absence of a structured way to articulate and visualize the plan, it is easy to talk past each other and overlook inconsistencies, contradictions, and disconnections.

Left unarticulated, contradicting visions don't conflict until after commitments are made and pieces are brought together. But when the strategy meets reality, details become disasters. At that late point, of course, the result is disagreement and waste:

disagreement about who misunderstood, overstepped, or is to blame; waste of both effort and time as teams race to rework, rejigger, and repatch the system.

Even when using these tools, there is still no guarantee that the blueprint you draw will be right. But by following the methodology in a dedicated, *team-based* effort, you can guarantee your best shot. Using a wide lens to harness and direct the collective insights of your partners makes falling victim to a blind spot far less likely. Having a disciplined approach at the beginning of a project allows you to see the impediments you'll eventually have to confront anyway. It shines a bright light on the path between you and your end customer. Modify the notion of "If we build it, will they come?" to instead ask, "If we build it, *how will they get here?*" You will want to know if the answer is, "We're not sure," before you commit your resources.

CHAPTER 5

Roles and Relationships:

To Lead or Follow in the Innovation Ecosystem?

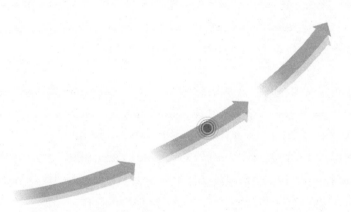

Succeeding in innovation ecosystems requires a clear, specific, plan for how the different elements and actors need to come together. This raises the question: who is responsible for bringing the plan to fruition? Who should take the reins and drive the endeavor, accepting the risks in an attempt to capture the glory and gains of leadership? When envisioning the relative profit and prestige of leaders like Intel, Microsoft, and Amazon, it is easy to conclude, "I want to lead." But wanting to lead and leading effectively are two different things.

Consider this story:* A senior manager from IBM and a senior manager from Oracle meet up with the owner of a midsize value-added reseller. They are all part of the same ecosystem—IBM and Oracle collaborate and compete in the information technology (IT) space, and the reseller has worked with both—and they get to talking about who is the leader. "Easy," says the man from IBM, "clearly, we are the leader here. We are the biggest, the most established, and have the largest network." The manager from Oracle counters, "You are the past and we are the future. We are growing our partner network faster and winning more business, so we are the leader." Finally, the reseller jumps in, "With all due respect, we are the leader. You guys make the products, but we guide the customers. We are the ones who influence who gets the sale, so we are the leader."

Who is the ecosystem leader in the story?

The answer is no one.

Yes, each plays an important part of the overall system, but being in the picture is not the same as being in charge of the picture. The leader is not the one who says, "I'm the leader." He's the one about whom *everyone else* says, "He's the leader." This is the litmus test of leadership and why no one in the story makes the grade: a "leader" without followers is just a guy in a suit.

Every participant in an ecosystem must ask himself whether he should lead or follow. Not, "Do I want to be the leader," but rather, "Is there a good reason that others would be willing to follow me?"

Creating followership among partnering firms entails more than just having a sound strategic vision or a great preexisting brand. These are all helpful, but they are not enough. In most cases, creating followership entails first making the up-front investments

---

* This is a caricature of a real exchange from a workshop I guided several years ago.

and taking the up-front risks required to get the system working, and only later reaping the rewards.

To be clear, ecosystem "leader" and "follower" do not map onto ecosystem "winner" and "loser." For the value proposition to succeed, everyone must win. The difference between leaders and followers is the way they win—the investment and risks they take up front, and the timing and size of their back-end payoffs.

The ecosystem leader's core challenge is creating a blueprint that creates value for the end user, assures that all necessary partners get enough surplus to warrant their participation, and leaves enough value in the end to make the leader's own efforts worthwhile.

What is the most difficult phrase in the sentence above?

In the end. Successful ecosystem leaders capture their outsized returns in the end, after the ecosystem is established and running. But in the beginning they build, sacrifice, and invest to ensure everyone else's participation.

Amazon creating the technology infrastructure and then subsidizing the publishers so that they would come aboard the Kindle effort; the movie studios finding a way to finance digital cinema systems for the exhibitors—there was no question who was leading in those cases, whose blueprint was being followed. Effective leadership demands not just an effective blueprint but also patience, a willingness to commit, and often (but not always) deep pockets as well. Without the means and desire to stay the course until your efforts reach fruition, you have nothing.

So who can lead? Who should lead? To help answer these questions I use a tool I call the *Leadership Prism*. It helps to clarify which actors in an ecosystem qualify for leadership contention and which actors should not bother wasting their resources on anything other than a (profitable) follower role. The leadership prism builds on the total-cost/relative-benefit logic of chapter 3 to assess the expected surplus of every actor in your value blueprint. It then

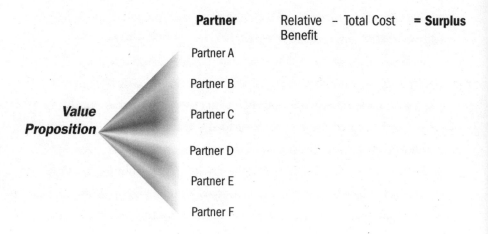

Figure 5.1: A generic leadership prism identifies all the actors in the ecosystem and the surplus they expect from participating.

considers which actor(s) has sufficient expected surplus to justify investing to offset whatever deficits exist in the system. It is only the actor(s) that meets these criteria that stands a credible chance of having the staying power to be the ecosystem leader.

To clarify the logic of leadership in an ecosystem, we will explore the multidecade effort to shift from error-prone paper-based medical records to electronic health records (EHRs). Our question is, who will be in a position to lead the EHR effort out of the tangle of co-innovation and adoption risk? It has taken nearly fifty years of false starts for the candidate to come to light. Who should lead?

Electronic Health Records

Each year, thousands of patient deaths are caused by avoidable medical errors in American hospitals. In 1999, the Institute of

Medicine famously estimated that number to be as high as 98,000. More recently, an April 2011 study from the Institute for Healthcare Improvement found that adverse events occur in one-third of hospital admissions—increasing the projections for avoidable harm. These medical errors can result from a variety of missteps—from infections caused by unwashed hands to mistakes made by overtired staff—but a great number are due to the archaic, paper-based record-keeping that, in 2010, was still in place in approximately 80 percent of American hospitals.

Adverse drug errors alone are estimated to harm 1.5 million people per year and kill several thousand, costing $3.5 billion annually. These medication missteps occur when prescriptions are hastily scribbled by a doctor—and then just as hastily read by a pharmacist. "It seems self-evident that many, perhaps most, of the solutions to medical mistakes will ultimately come through better information technology," said Dr. Robert Wachter, chief of the UCSF Medical Center in 2004.

In a $2 trillion industry (the largest in the United States) that is in many ways technology driven, health care's reliance on paper and pen to document patient records is all the more surprising. Other information-intensive industries invest 10 percent of their revenues on IT, but the health-care industry spends only 2 percent. So why is it that we can have our brains scanned by a state-of-the-art MRI machine and our faulty heartbeats regulated by pacemakers that can wirelessly transmit updates on our cardiac status, but we must still rely on the pharmacist's best guess at the doctor's scribbled drug prescription?

Health-care insiders, pioneering technology companies, and policy makers have been discussing a digital alternative to paper-based medical records since the 1950s. Besides the obvious benefit of improved safety, studies show a gain of nearly 30 percent efficiency through the reduction of paperwork (the average physician fills out more than 20,000 forms each year) and unnecessary or redundant tests. Ultimately, according to senior researchers at the RAND Corporation, "the adoption of interoperable EMR [electronic medical record] systems could produce efficiency and safety savings of \$142–\$371 billion."

For the health IT sector, the successful implementation of electronic health records is an enormous opportunity. Over the years players big and small have devoted massive resources to finding a way to implement EHR in the health-care industry—but have mostly left a wreckage of false starts. Why?

Using the leadership prism we can identify the source of the breakdown as well as the path to a solution.

The first electronic health records emerged in the late 1960s. Larry Weed at the University of Vermont began one of the earliest attempts, dubbed PROMIS (problem-oriented medical information system). This was soon followed by similar efforts across the country at a small number of hospitals and universities giving rise to a sea of acronyms. In Salt Lake City, LDS (Latter-Day Saints) Hospital developed HELP (health evaluation through logical processing), and in Boston, Massachusetts General Hospital created COSTAR (Computer Stored Ambulatory Record). Leading companies from IBM to 3M and new entrants like HBOC (later purchased by McKesson) and SMS (now part of Siemens Corporation) also invested heavily toward the goal. But despite early enthusiasm and investment, this first wave of electronic health records failed to spark the revolution. While the early deployments at pioneering hospitals showed that the benefits of EHR were real, the technology hurdles were simply too great to make meaningful progress: computers were unwieldy, processing expensive, and storage difficult to maintain. Expectations for widespread adoption and efficiency gains crashed on the shoals of co-innovation risk, resulting in huge write-offs, exits, and continued systemwide inefficiency.

By the year 2000, many of the technology challenges standing in the way of electronic medical records had been solved. On the hardware front, everything from microprocessors, memory, and computer screens were light-years ahead of where they had been during earlier efforts. The cheapest, worst-performing laptop in 2000 was orders of magnitude more powerful than the best multi-story mainframes of the 1960s and 1970s.

For proponents of EHR, the most important change was the widespread adoption of the Internet, which enabled easy transfer and communication of records. The largest technology compa-nies all sensed an opportunity in the space and invested millions developing electronic health records solutions in various capaci-ties. By the mid-1990s, IBM was again involved in EHR develop-ment on several fronts. The company's Pre-Scribe network, which gives pharmacies the capability for electronic prescriptions, was employed by more than 5,000 pharmacies by 1997. Its Health Data Network Express, announced in 1998, was a Web-based system that recorded and saved information a patient would share with a nurse when calling with a health issue. Furthering its mission to find an IT solution for health-care organizations, IBM teamed up with several providers in the early 2000s—including Kaiser Per-manente, an HMO with nearly 9 million members—to digitize patient records.

Intel, the leader in computer chips, also entered the EHR game as the century got going. In 2006, it joined forces with several other blue-chip companies (Wal-Mart, Intel, Pitney Bowes, Applied Materials, British Petroleum, and Cardinal Health) to create Dos-sia, an employer-led program that planned to provide electronic health records for more than 2.5 million people. "It's time to modernize the health care system," exclaimed Intel chairman Craig Barrett.

Simultaneous efforts by several health IT specialists also furthered EHR development. Epic Systems Corporation, founded in 1979, created and deployed software in midsize and large healthcare organizations. Cerner Corporation, another entrant, offered software and support for practices seeking digital solutions. Medical equipment giants GE, Siemens, and Toshiba entered with their own IT offerings.

On the consumer end, in 2007, Microsoft entered the picture with the launch of HealthVault, a free Web-based health records system that patients themselves control. The idea was that patients would be empowered to manage their own medical records and ultimately give doctors, clinics, and hospitals (who agreed to partner with Microsoft) permission to access and update their medical records. Google Health, a similar offering, entered the field the following year but, in frustration, discontinued its service after 2011.

These efforts were well funded, numerous, and varied—targeting hospitals, departments, employers, patients, and health systems. And yet, even with this diversity of approaches and intensity of effort, as late as 2009 only 9 percent of U.S. hospitals had implemented electronic health records systems. And even among those facilities equipped with the technology, actual use was well below potential. Why?

A Someday, One-Day Proposition

As the co-innovation hurdles to electronic health records were finally disappearing, lives were going to be saved—and money was going to be made. So why did EHR begin to gain serious momentum only in 2011? The answer lies in recognizing what, beyond technology, is required to actually put electronic health records into operation in a hospital setting. And no less important, in identifying who has the means—and the will—to lead such a massive change effort.

A hospital is an unwieldy organization, a complex array of care-giving, economics, and branding. For a hospital to embrace an entirely new system of record-keeping, a chain of adopters would have to sign on—administrators, department heads, and medical staff—each with its own unique way of examining the costs and benefits of the EHR proposition. (Note that, for the sake of clarity, I am presenting a simplified ecosystem here. Adding the myriad complexities of the U.S. health-care system to include lobbyists, regulators, standards bodies, and the host of other ecosystem participants would make the analysis more complicated but would affect neither the message nor method.)

What would the cost and benefit look like for the partners in this adoption chain? (I will offer illustrative numbers drawn from a scale of 1 to 10 to clarify the intuition.)

For the IT provider, the answer is straightforward: a big up-front investment in developing the EHR system and a costly sales and deployment process at every client site could yield a big reward

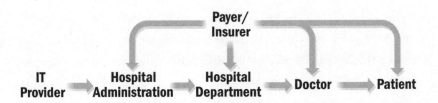

Figure 5.2: A simplified adoption chain for electronic health records (excludes regulators, standards bodies, etc.).

in the form of a hefty sales price ($20 million to $50 million is not out of line for a large hospital), as well as the promise of recurring revenue for system maintenance and updates (on the order of 20 to 25 percent per year). *Cost is high: 5. Benefit is higher: 8. Surplus: +3.*

For the hospital's administration, the benefits of EHR are abundantly clear: with this system in place, thousands of errors can be avoided, leading to a reduction of complications, costs, and even deaths. Indeed, the promise of EHR converges perfectly with the pillar of medical ethics: *primum non nocere*, "first do no harm." And while clinicians are the ones who take this oath, the philosophy permeates the system.

Price is an issue, of course. Setting up an electronic health records system is an expensive proposition, requiring retraining of all staff and constant maintenance costs. The direct costs are evident. And the indirect costs—training, project management, change management, customization—can be nearly double the initial outlay. Despite the expense, though, most administrators will agree: the benefits of lives saved and efficiencies gained exceed the cost. And in today's competitive environment, health-care providers are eager to be perceived as technologically innovative.

Even so, the hospital administrators have had a hard time signing on the dotted line. Why? First, although everyone initially agrees that EHR is an exciting idea, they start to wonder: How else could that $40 million be spent to improve patient care? What about training the staff to wash their hands before and after every patient encounter? After all, poor hand hygiene contributes to the high rates of infections acquired in hospitals that, according to the World Health Organization, kill more than 90,000 patients per year globally. What about giving overworked nurses—that crucial first line in patient care—more time off? Or more training?

Or purchasing the latest-generation imaging machine to diagnose brain tumors and other hard-to-spot cancers? There are countless ways to increase the quality of patient care, many of which seem more enticing than an invisible IT system. Dr. Russell Ricci, then general manager of global health care industry at IBM, expressed frustration at the pace of adoption: "The Institute of Medicine study says that we kill 100,000 people a year with hospital errors. Yet most of the hospitals still do not have an electronic point-of-care order-entry system. With it, that number of errors would never happen. But instead of investing in that, many hospitals are out building new buildings or buying new M.R.I.'s."

This issue of opportunity cost—what other value proposition could I purchase for the same price?—is only the first problem. The second is the assurance of no "opportunity lost." The administrators know that the opportunity to adopt EHR isn't going to disappear. Not only will the EHR sales rep be back, but she'll be back with a better and possibly cheaper system. Compounding this hesitation is the regulatory uncertainty inherent to any new technology. Why take on the "first adopter disadvantage" for a product that may not have worked out all the kinks? What if some other system becomes the standard in a few years, and they have to scrap the whole thing and start over? Frustratingly for the sales rep, the administrators never say, "No, thanks. We don't want digital records. Leave and never come back." Instead, they say, "Now isn't the right time. Let's look again next year."

But some administrators will be convinced of the need for immediate action. For academic and research-focused facilities, because of their pioneering approach to health-care solutions, the benefits of EHR often outweigh the total costs. Breaking new ground is a central mission of these health-care providers, thus the value of EHR is heightened. The Mayo Clinic, University of

Pittsburgh Medical Center, and the Dartmouth-Hitchcock Medical Center were early adopters, launching pilots and deploying systems—often homegrown—in the 1990s, as was the Veterans Health Administration, whose mandate and size both increased the attractiveness of EHR. *Cost is significant: 4. Benefit is higher: 6. Surplus: +2.*

But even a procurement order and the support of top management are not enough to reap the benefit of digitized health records. Hospitals are divided up into administrative (billing, records) and medical departments (pediatrics, orthopedics, radiology, etc.), all of whom must come on board for the promise of EHR to be fulfilled. And why wouldn't they? EHR means that communication within and among these various departments will be more efficient and less error prone. With patient records available in real time, with the click of a button, handoffs among departments are streamlined; intake and discharge are seamless. But as our intrepid sales rep trudges from department to department, she is met with the same answer: "Communicating with all the other departments sounds great. I love it. Come back to me just as soon you have everyone else on board." It is the rare department that wants to be the one to pioneer EHR in its organization—especially if it needs to fund the transition from its own budgets.

Some departments, like billing and radiology, tend to stand out in their willingness to embrace digital records. As the middleman between insurers and patients, billing is a paperwork jungle, so going digital means a more streamlined workflow. For radiologists—doctors who analyze X-rays, CAT scans, and MRIs—EHR offers an especially high value proposition. First, these images are expensive to print, and digital files cut costs. (Because X-rays contain silver, a month's worth of blank X-rays can cost upward of $50,000 for an active radiology center.) Second, the ability to send images across town—or the world—for a second opinion on a time-sensitive case can save lives. Third is the improved quality of life that EHR offers—radiologists no longer have to head to the hospital for emergency calls at 3 a.m. Now they can read images from their home offices in their pajamas. As of 2009, 78 percent of hospitals were enabled with electronic radiology reports. *Cost: 2. Benefit: 3. Surplus: +1.*

But even departmental sign-off is not enough for EHR's benefits to be realized. Nothing will happen unless and until the health-care practitioners themselves begin using the system. Radiologists have been the exception. In the typical scenario, the co-opted department heads call a meeting with their respective staffs. "Going digital is going to be great," they'll say. "You'll each reach a higher level of performance, and patient safety will increase." For the doctors and nurses, this sounds well and good except for the fact that the onus is on them to learn and use the new system. Transitioning from paper-based patient records to a digital system is not a simple endeavor. Training takes weeks, not days, which means the staff will not be able to see patients while they are learning the new computer systems, and therefore no money will be coming into the facility.

Even with training, doctors know that those first weeks or months back on the job are going to be rough. One estimate predicts doctor productivity dipping 20 percent for the first three to six months after EHR implementation. There is a learning curve involved with any new skill, and the promise of heightened productivity will seem a distant prospect as they stand in the hallway while their patients wait, trying to find the right pull-down menu for a patient's varied medical history.

For most doctors, the relative benefit of a digital over a paper-based system is slim to none. Sure, theoretically, EHR sounds good, but no doctor sees himself as the problem. Is there any surprise that an overscheduled doctor who spends his days talking to patients, interpreting, diagnosing, and operating sees note-taking as the trivial part of the job? And since doctors are not the ones who tend to handle the reams of paperwork that make a hospital function, nor the ones who must interpret their own handwriting to fill prescriptions, their motivation to change is low. At the same time, their opportunity cost is high since they feel their time would be better spent learning the latest medical advancements instead of becoming data entry clerks. While doctors agree with the theoretical benefits of EHR, they see them as unjustified given the opportunity cost. And in small practices, where doctors bear the IT expenses more directly, the proposition looks even more negative. *Cost: 3. Benefit: 1. Surplus: –2.*

Who Will Lead in EHR?

Without a clear leader in place, EHR faces an exasperating paradox: most actors in the health-care provider ecosystem will always want it, but no one will ever be ready for it. At the beginning of the chapter, I introduced the leadership prism as a tool to help us assess the net gains to each party in any development effort and whether or not anyone has sufficient surplus to be the ecosystem leader. Let's take a look at the EHR leadership prism below and briefly examine how each party views the cost and benefit of going digital.

For the IT provider, while the cost of developing EHR is quite substantial, the benefit is huge. After all, health care is the leading industry in the United States, so any firm that captures even a small piece of the EHR pie is going to see substantial profits. IT gains a sizable surplus (surplus: +3). For the hospital administrations, there is some surplus but not as much as that for information technology. The benefit of reducing errors is of course significant. Then again, so is the cost of implementation (surplus: +2). The

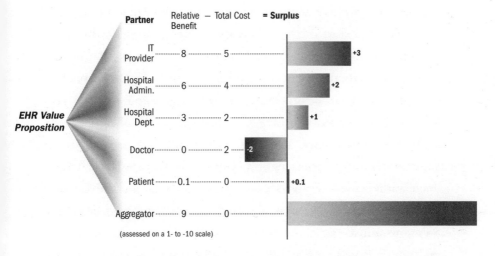

Figure 5.3: Leadership prism for electronic health records (EHRs) at a hospital with example values for relative benefit and total cost for each partner.

individual departments will see some benefit from the added efficiency EHR will bring. But hospital-wide implementation will be difficult and slow, given that the departments are fragmented (surplus: +1). Finally, for the doctors, the benefits of EHR are low, but the cost of adoption is high, given the time lost to training followed by lowered efficiency—leading to a deficit (surplus: –2).

And where does the patient—health care's raison d'être—fall in the EHR leadership prism? Is it possible that patients themselves can lead us out of the dark ages of pen and paper? Certainly, the patient bears no (direct) cost for the EHR effort, so shouldn't he be a huge advocate for the system? No. On an individual level, statistics mean very little. Most people who go into a hospital believe they will once again see the light of day. Moreover, most people who pick up a prescription from the pharmacy don't view the transaction as putting their lives at risk. Consider the numbers: even if medication errors kill thousands of people each year, that represents only a tiny fraction of a total of 3.9 billion prescriptions filled. The probability of any one individual coming to any harm due to medical error is akin to winning the lottery (though considerably less appealing). *Cost: 0. Benefit: 0.1. Surplus: 0.1.* The individual patient sees no meaningful surplus here.

Recalling the adoption chain methodology from chapter 3, the doctors in our EHR effort are at a clear minus. It takes only one negative to undermine an endeavor, so without an ecosystem leader who can turn that negative into a positive, electronic health records will remain a pipe dream. One might assume that IT, with its large surplus, would be in a position to take the reins. But even Microsoft and Google, who each launched their own Web-based health records systems in 2007 and 2008, respectively, have failed to move the market forward in a significant way. And, as for Intel's efforts, according to Colin Evans, the director of policy and standards at Intel's digital health group, "We underestimated the challenges." In the context of the leadership prism, we clearly see that if they were to allocate their surplus to offset the doctors' deficit, they themselves would hardly break even.

Where is the great value promised by the transition to EHR? Where is the huge surplus from all those lives saved? Without an actor who can find it, and deploy it to shift the doctors into surplus, nothing will happen.

If the ecosystem includes just the five traditional players, EHR will remain an academic dream. The answer, then, requires introducing a new player—an aggregator. Because the odds of mistakes are so low, the benefits of EHR are invisible to the individual patient. They become material only when we aggregate outcomes over a large enough number of patients. We need to find an actor whose surplus is affected by patients not as individuals but as a group, and who is able to both capture and distribute this benefit; insurers, health-care systems, and governments all fit the bill. And the larger the group, the larger the surplus.

For example, the Veterans Health Administration (VHA) is the largest medical organization in the United States, serving over 8.5 million veterans at 1,100 facilities. It employs the Veterans Health Information Systems and Technology Architecture (VISTA), an EHR solution that is one of the largest used in the world. The system is credited with reforming a health-care system mired in substandard safety and efficiency. While up to 8 percent of prescriptions in the United States are filled incorrectly, the VHA has an error rate of just 0.003 percent. In the private sector, Kaiser Permanente operates the largest privately deployed EHR solution in the world, linking 36 hospitals and 454 medical offices to coordinate the care of 8.6 million patients.

Biggest of all, of course, are governments. In the United States, the federal government stepped into the picture in 2009 with the passage of the Health Information Technology for Economic and Clinical Health Act, legislation to promote EHR. Ironically, for twenty years the IT industry had lobbied for the government to stay out of the EHR game. With dollar signs in their eyes, they assumed any government intervention could only hurt their bottom line. But after years of stalled efforts, the industry changed its approach, clamoring for someone to create a law to enforce EHR adoption.

The Obama administration allocated substantial funding ($27 billion, compared to the prior administration's $50 million) to the EHR effort, the vast majority of which will be used to incentivize doctors and hospitals. These incentives are in the form of increased Medicare and Medicaid payments for "meaningful use of certified EHR systems" that start high and decrease over time. This legislation calls for doctors who buy and use EHR systems to receive up to $44,000, spread over five years through Medicare, or up to $63,750 over six years from Medicaid. Then, in 2015, these carrots turn to sticks when doctors who have not adopted EHR "meaningfully" (consistently updating digital records with diagnoses, monitoring drug interactions, and ordering prescriptions) will see their payments cut.

To be sure, a variety of concerns remain about the true benefits that will be gained through EHR—from implementation problems to privacy risks to the daunting challenge of creating cross-platform compatibility across what are currently closed and proprietary IT systems. What is clear, however, is that with the current structure of the EHR ecosystem, large aggregators are the only parties with enough surplus to lead. Deep pockets, along with a willingness on the part of the government to prioritize the effort, mean that electronic health records will finally have a chance to gain traction outside the academic sphere.

The EHR case offers a powerful demonstration of the leadership prism at work. The ecosystem struggled for years as IT providers tried to compete and differentiate in a setting where a critical link in the adoption chain was broken. In the absence of a credible ecosystem leader—one with sufficient benefit to bring everyone into surplus—meaningful progress was impossible.

The leadership prism logic helps explain the contrast between the successes of digital cinema and of Amazon in e-books, on the one hand, and the failures of Michelin's run-flats and Sony's attempt at e-book leadership, on the other. Beyond a vision and a blueprint, leadership requires a willingness to sacrifice and an ability to induce followership. It is not for everyone.

The Case for Followership

The temptation to grab the leadership torch is powerful. Who wouldn't want to call the shots so they can win big every time? The leadership prism should help put those urges in perspective. The reality is, no one has pockets deep enough to finance every endeavor.

Ask Microsoft in television set-top boxes, Intel in WiMAX mobile communication, and Wal-Mart in radio frequency identification (RFID) chips for consumer packaged goods. Ask every IT player in EHR: only when they chose to follow (and support) the government's lead was real progress—and money—made. No one will stop you from spending a fortune on a leadership candidacy you can't win. You can try to lead in every ecosystem where you play, or you can choose to be involved only in leading ecosystems. The latter, smarter, option means that sometimes you will be a follower.

For ecosystem followers, smaller up-front commitments mean a smaller downside risk. In contrast to a leader, who invests early and profits late, a follower's required investment is lower and more quickly recovered. And whereas the ecosystem leader must juggle the nine balls that are the key followers while simultaneously maintaining discipline within his own organization, the follower need only manage his one. By definition, any successful ecosystem is filled with followers who win. Their piece of the pie may be smaller than that of the leader, but then again, they bear a much smaller risk. For the leader to win, followers have to win too. There is a lot to like.

A Checklist for Smart Followership

So, if you aren't in a position to lead, whom should you follow? It's likely there will be a multitude of leadership candidates wooing you. This is what gives followers their leverage. If you have an element that companies X, Y, and Z all need to further their competing value propositions, whose ecosystem should you grace with your participation?

First, assess the quality of their plan. What are the co-innovation risks—not just those that touch you directly but across the entire design? What is the adoption chain? Where are you positioned, and what do the surplus balances reveal? Draw out the complete value blueprint to see what the color scheme is. And then, no less crucial than your own assessment, confirm that the ecosystem leader sees the blueprint the same way you do. It could be that he sees things you don't. But it may also be that he has a major blind spot that hasn't been accounted for, in which case you know to either consult or keep looking.

Second, for the blueprints that are sound, construct a leadership prism. This will reveal how much each potential leader has at stake in the endeavor. Which candidate's surplus is sufficient to make a real go of it, subsidizing others when necessary and funding the effort for the long haul? They will all tell you, "We'll do everything to make this ecosystem work." But, at best, what they really mean is, "We'll do everything *we can* to make this ecosystem work." Their expected surplus is the hard upper bound on the resources—money, labor, time, commitment—the leadership candidates can make available. With a clear eye on the balance of surpluses and deficits across each plan, you can then assess whether, given the size of their resource base and their own expected surplus, they are really able and willing to afford the price required to turn all the red lights green.

Third, the smart follower will probe the details of the win-win proposition: Do they make money when I win? Do I make money when they win? Expect problems unless you can reply with two definitive yeses. This question is crucial because it helps you avoid signing on for an opportunity that may seem fruitful on the surface but is undermined from the outset by misaligned incentives. Recall the Sony/Amazon discussion from chapter 4. One of the reasons the publishers found it easier to follow Amazon's lead was that they recognized a commonality: just as publishers make their money by selling individual books, so too does Amazon. Sony, on the other hand, is primarily a hardware company, banking on its

Reader device to drive profits. The follow-on sale of individual books is of much lower concern to them (a fact that is also true of Apple's priorities in the e-book ecosystem).

Fourth, while leadership can be lonely, followership can quickly get crowded. Ask yourself: Who else is in the room? Whom will I be competing with? The pace of today's technological advancements means that many companies gather a slew of competing followers into a specific ecosystem. While the leader waits to see who writes the best and fastest code, or who creates the most effective diagnostic tests, rival followers sweat to create the better product for a lower price. Exclusivity, or at the very least a reduction of competitive pressures within an ecosystem, is a factor that may be worth fighting for.

Every innovation effort will involve some uncertainty for both leaders and followers. For the latter, this insecurity is compounded by a lack of control. Will this plan—constructed and implemented by someone else—work? Will I get my promised share? And, how long can I stay before the leader starts squeezing my surplus? When a follower's position becomes too attractive, too critical, or too easy to assume, it can be very tempting for the leader to step in with its own competing effort, cutting the follower out of the ecosystem. The evolving relationship between Amazon and traditional book publishers is telling in this regard. The attractive leadership candidate is aligned with your goals but doesn't overlap with your activities.

We are all navigating through an imperfect world. But with eyes wide open, we can make more informed choices.

Leadership Revisited

Leadership in any arena is rarely uncontested. In the race to win, an ecosystem leader must act fast, enticing critical followers early on, ensuring the effort gains momentum. And, in order to appeal to these partners, leaders need to have an understanding of how potential followers will be evaluating their proposition. This ability to see your offering from the perspective of followers is crucial; it is the key to creating effective enticements to get them, and keep them, on board.

Remember: the litmus test for leadership is that *everyone else* agrees to follow—which only happens when everyone else wins too. An effective leader creates the ecosystem's structure, establishes fair standards and consistency, and convinces potential followers that there is value in it for them. We have already encountered examples of effective ecosystem leadership in earlier chapters.

The first was the case of digital cinema. In order for digital cinema to reach audiences, the expensive systems would have to be installed in theaters across the country. Who was going to pay the high costs up front? Not the theater owners, who saw a big minus in the digital cinema adoption chain. So, for a decade, digital cinema was stagnant. In an example of effective inducement, the studios finally took the reins of the digital cinema effort by creating the virtual print fee system, creating a financing bridge to enable the installation of the digital system in thousands of movie theaters across the country. It was a big up-front commitment but a bargain for a leader with a long time horizon. Remember: the leader usually captures value in the end. Moreover, in the end, the studios stand to capture huge savings as they phase out expensive prints and shipping costs in favor of cheaper digital files. And the structure they built, with an explicit expiration date for the virtual print fee payments, should help maintain an atmosphere of trust and fairness as they eventually reduce the subsidy.

In another instance of smart leadership, Amazon brought e-books to mainstream readers by leveraging its retail power in an ecosystem where it played a crucial center role. Amazon kept all the players aligned as it headed toward the ultimate goal of offering a seamless e-book solution. Furthering its mission, Amazon eased the transition by sacrificing its share of e-book margins in order to subsidize the publishers. It wasn't the Kindle device that launched e-books, it was Amazon's effective ecosystem leadership that pushed the effort forward.

Ultimately, in a successful ecosystem, leaders and followers both prosper. Either position holds the promise of winning. The worst-case scenario: being a leader that loses. No one is going to stop you from throwing good money into a bad plan. It falls on you to prioritize where you want to lead, whom you want to follow, and—if neither choice is appealing—when to opt out and wait for a better opportunity.

CHAPTER 6

The Right Place and the Right Time:

When Does the Early Bird Get the Worm?

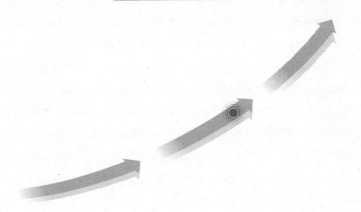

Beyond envisioning what to bring together and how to bring it together, *when* do you bring all the elements of your great vision together? There is a window of opportunity for every innovation. For many managers, the siren song of early-mover advantage can seem irresistible. After all, being early means unobstructed access to the market, the ability to establish an industry standard, not to mention free publicity and the resulting brand recognition that can create lasting privilege with customers. Early movers such as Amazon (online retail), Xerox (copiers), and eBay (online auctions) enjoyed all these tantalizing advantages and, to this day, lead their respective industries.

Although conventional wisdom applauds the pursuit of early-mover advantage, the complexity of innovation ecosystems can overturn this logic. The usual focus on getting products to market creates a dangerous blind spot when it comes to timing entry: the early bird may get the worm, but the second mouse gets the cheese.

In this chapter we will explore the different implications of being a pioneer or a late entrant, directly linking performance to where in the ecosystem your biggest challenges lie. If the biggest obstacle is overcoming the execution challenge, getting to market before your rivals can create great advantage. But in a world of dependencies, the benefit of preempting the competition is directly related to your co-innovators' readiness with their offerings. If co-innovators are late (recall Nokia's long, disastrous wait for 3G partners), striving to be first can be pointless or, worse, detrimental to your effort. You may be the driver that races ahead just to wait at the red light alongside everyone else. Given the complexities of innovation ecosystems, simply asking yourself if you should be an early or late entrant will no longer suffice. The smarter question now is: *under what circumstances* should I be early or late?

To embark upon our exploration, consider the evolution of the portable music player industry. At first glance, it defies logic. In 1979, Sony's pioneering Walkman, the world's first portable cassette player, was able to benefit from a first-mover advantage that lasted over thirty years. However, with the same customer set and value proposition, the world's first portable MP3 player, SaeHan's MPMan, introduced in 1998, enjoyed no early-mover advantage. It was Apple, which launched its iPod *three years after* the first mover, that finally dominated the industry. How did this happen?

First Mover: Advantage or Disadvantage?

In 1978, engineers at Sony successfully married a compact play-back device with lightweight headphones to create the prototype for a product that would become a worldwide hit. In 1979, the Walkman was introduced in the Japanese market, selling out its entire production run within the first three months. Combining a technology based on a previous innovation—Sony's Pressman recorder, a pricey device aimed primarily at journalists—with an aggressive marketing campaign targeting a young demographic, Sony pioneered the market. Consumers, already accustomed to playing cassettes on boom boxes and car stereos, were eager to emulate the happy youths of Sony's ads—roller-skating, picnicking, and jogging, all while listening to their favorite music.

Soon Sanyo, Panasonic, Sharp, Philips, and other electronics leaders joined the fray. Some rival products boasted additional features like AM/FM radio, water resistance, and recording capabilities, but none captured the popular imagination of the Walkman.

For a decade after its launch, Sony's Walkman retained a 50 percent market share in the United States (46 percent in Japan) in a space teeming with competitors, even as it enjoyed a price premium of approximately $20 over rival offers. Showcasing the power of first-mover advantage, Sony's pioneering technology set the benchmark for everything that came after it. And the media's hyperfocus on the Walkman meant that followers were seen as mere imitation. Like Kleenex, Band-Aid, and Xerox, the Walkman name became the catchall term for an entire product category.

Jump ahead to the late 1990s, when the sun had set on cassettes as the preferred music delivery format in favor of compact discs and, for the technologically savvy, digital MP3 files. So too did the Walkman's relevance begin to fade in favor of Sony's follow-up device, the Discman. But electronics firms around the globe were betting that the compact disc would soon follow the cassette into extinction. Who was going to capitalize on the rise of the MP3? Which MP3 player would get there first and become the next Walkman?

In 1998, South Korea's SaeHan Information Systems created the world's first portable digital audio player, MPMan. That summer, the handheld MPMan, boasting 32 MB of memory and initially priced at $350 (a 64 MB version retailed for $500), was launched in the United States. MPMan was soon joined by a panoply of first-generation MP3 players from established firms as well as start-ups. Diamond Multimedia's Rio PMP300, less pricey at $199, led the way a few months after MPMan's launch, followed by Compaq/HanGo's Personal Jukebox. The next year, Creative Technology introduced its Nomad, and Sensory Science launched Rave. In 2000, Samsung and Sony both joined the race. The offerings varied in both design and capacity. (Most notably, the Personal Jukebox, launched just months after MPMan, was the first MP3 player to use a hard drive rather than a flash drive, enabling it to increase capacity to a then unheard-of 6 GB.) By the launch of the iPod in 2001, there were approximately fifty portable MP3 players available in the United States—and no firm had achieved anywhere near the dominance that the Walkman had enjoyed twenty years earlier. Although IDC predicted sales of MP3 players to reach 9 million by 2006, unit sales in 2001 were only 248,000.

SaeHan saw the market, delivered the product, embraced the right file format, and did it all before the competition. But unlike Sony, it did not enjoy a first-mover advantage. Why was first-mover advantage so large in the portable music player industry in one technology generation but completely absent in another?

First, we must ask: what does it take for a portable music player to create value? By design, these devices are basic; a customer need only add batteries and the music itself. For the Walkman, this was simple. Cassettes had been in wide use in home and car stereos since 1972. And by 1979, retailers in every town and every city sold them alongside vinyl records.

But in 1998, the story was very different for MP3s. You couldn't purchase them in traditional retail settings, and although the press had begun sounding the recording industry's copyright fears, the reality was that few people were actually illegally downloading songs off the Web. Remember 28.8 Kbps dial-up modems? Downloading an album—legally or not—could be a multihour affair, punctuated by the frustration of dropped connections.

In 1998, the world was on the verge of the Internet bubble, but it wasn't quite there yet. At the time, Christopher Mines of Forrester Research predicted: "Once consumers get a taste of high-speed Internet access at home, they'll never go back to dial-up." He was right, but most people hadn't tasted broadband yet, meaning illegally downloading music was a time-consuming process mainly embarked upon by tech-savvy college students. Few adults who could actually afford the $200–$300 MP3 players were going to spend hours painstakingly building their MP3 collection through downloads or transferring songs from their well-stocked CD racks. According to the digital rights management team a2b, "Currently the only protection mechanism in place for CDs is the sheer bulk of the data. Until the bandwidth available to most consumers increases, it will be cumbersome to move even compressed CDs around."

While portable cassette players could create value as soon as they were launched due to the widespread availability of cassettes, MP3 players were not able to truly create value until the content was broadly available. The MPMan and its kin may have gotten there early, but they faced crucial co-innovation challenges that stymied mass adoption. It didn't matter that MPMan was first—it wouldn't have mattered if it was sixth, twenty-third, or forty-second. Without the extensive access to MP3s and broadband, the value proposition could not come together.

The iPod Wins, Three Years Late

The MP3 player market did eventually consolidate around a dominant product, Apple's iPod. But the iPod, launched in late 2001—three years after the MPMan—was anything but a first mover. How can we understand the iPod's success despite its delayed entry?

In 1997, the late Steve Jobs returned to Apple, the company he had co-founded as a college dropout, as interim CEO. As the Internet bubble grew, Apple was hungry for growth. Only a sliver of computer users had embraced its Mac offering. In 2001, Jobs noted: "Apple has about 5 percent market share today. Most of the other 95 percent of computer buyers don't even consider us."

Jobs was a pioneer of the convergence of digital and media. It is inconceivable that digital music was not on his radar. Still, in Jobs's early tenure as CEO, and despite his company's need to create a new avenue for growth, he refused to jump on the MP3 bandwagon. Asked in 1998 about his growth strategy, "Jobs just smiled and said, 'I am going to wait for the next big thing.'" In 1998, as MPMan and others launched, he didn't budge. In 1999, as Shawn Fanning introduced Napster (illegally), unleashing a vast catalog of free MP3 content to the world, Jobs still didn't move. In 2000, Jobs finally decided to start the process of developing an MP3 player.

In 2001, the bubble burst, and in the bleak outlook for all things Internet related the MP3 player was not spared. As a spokeswoman at Intel sadly noted, "With some of the consumers we have talked to, it sure seems like things are slowing down in the MP3 player market." It was at this dreary moment that Steve Jobs finally launched his player in the market. Why? What had he been waiting for? What did he know?

Jobs knew that, on its own, an MP3 player was useless. He understood that, in order for the device to have value, other co-innovators in the MP3 player ecosystem first needed to be aligned. And in October 2001, when Apple announced the iPod, those pieces were solidly in place: both MP3s and broadband were finally widely available.

Apple waited, and then waited some more—until it finally made its move, putting the last two pieces in place to create a winning innovation: an attractive, simple device supported by smart software. The first-generation iPod for Macintosh retailed at $399, had 5 GB capacity, and could store up to 1,000 songs. It boasted an intuitive interface design and was, for its time, lightweight. But the value of the device was cemented by its seamlessness with the iTunes music management software. Organizing and managing your MP3s was finally a breeze. But unlike other MP3 players, which used a USB cable to transfer music files from computer to device, the iPod relied on a faster, built-in FireWire port, a standard feature on all newer Macs but available on only a fraction of PCs. (FireWire was a favorite feature of Jobs's, given that it is significantly faster than USB—users could transfer 1,000 songs in less than ten minutes.)

Despite being available only for Mac users, the iPod was the fastest-selling MP3 player to ever hit the market. That first holiday season saw 125,000 units sold. Analysts called it "the hit of the holiday season," "revolutionary," and "brilliant." In March 2002, Apple doubled the iPod's disk capacity with a 10 GB offering and in July announced the much-anticipated Windows-compatible iPod. Sales were on the rise: by the end of the year, consumers had purchased over 600,000 iPods. Still, Apple held only 15 percent of the digital player market.

In April 2003, Apple announced the iTunes Music Store, an online retail hub where customers could browse and purchase music for $0.99 per song (or $9.99 per album). Crucially, Apple's stringent FairPlay digital rights management system meant that record labels could finally breathe easy that the intellectual property of their artists would be protected. And, iPod users could hold their heads up high knowing that their music was (at least potentially) legally acquired. "Consumers don't want to be treated like criminals, and artists don't want their valuable work stolen. The iTunes Music Store offers a groundbreaking solution for both," Jobs stated. The iPod, of course, still did an excellent job of playing pirated content as well.

At launch, the iTunes Store had a collection of 200,000 songs from major labels such as BMG, EMI, Sony Music Entertainment, Universal, and Warner. In its first week, Apple sold over 1 million songs. By 2005, its library had grown to 1.5 million songs. Although Apple would make scant profit from selling songs at $0.99 (it had sold nearly 8 billion songs by the end of 2009, but with an estimated operating margin of 10 percent on song sales, that translates to only $800 million in operating profits over six years—trivial when compared to its earnings from the over 220 million iPods it had sold by 2009), the iTunes store gave the iPod legitimacy in a world of shady MP3 downloads.

Soon after the launch of the iTunes store, Apple released an iPod that was compatible with both FireWire and USB cables, opening up its best-selling device to the entire world of PC users. It was at this point that Apple cemented its dominance.

According to NPD Group, sales of portable CD players were still more than double those of MP3 players during the holiday season of 2004. But between the third quarters of 2004 and 2005, sales of the iPod had leaped 616 percent.

As the years passed, Apple kept on innovating. The iPod became sleeker, smaller; it had more and more memory. For consumers, this meant there was always a fresher, more appealing iPod to own. As the same customer base kept repurchasing new and better iPods, Apple's profits soared: by 2008 it had captured 48 percent of the MP3 player market share. SanDisk's Sansa MP3 player was the iPod's closest competitor with 8 percent market share.

Few would deny that the iPod is a great product, surpassing any other MP3 player offering. But is it six times better? Why is it that this technology succeeded to such a great extent where others—established, smart others—barely made any progress at all? Apple was, after all, three years late. But perhaps this logic should be flipped: perhaps everyone else was three years too early. As we'll see again in chapter 8 when we explore the iPhone, Jobs tended to be late for everything because he wanted everything to be ready for him. Reflecting on catching technology waves in 2008, he said, "Things happen fairly slowly, you know. They do. These waves of technology, you can see them way before they happen, and you just have to choose wisely which ones you're going to surf. If you choose unwisely, then you can waste a lot of energy, but if you choose wisely, it actually unfolds fairly slowly. It takes years." Jobs's discipline paid off. In the three years between the launch of the MPMan and the iPod, each element in the MP3 player ecosystem turned from red to green. Instead of waiting at the red light with everyone else—wasting precious resources and time—Apple drove right on through a green light toward victory, becoming, according to the *Economist*, "the Walkman of the early 21st century."

Early-Mover Advantage in Products vs. Ecosystems

When we think about early-mover advantages we tend to think in product terms. The outsize profits of winning exemplars—Birds Eye in frozen foods, Xerox in copiers, Intel in microprocessors, Bayer in aspirin, and DuPont in nylon—are held up as proof of the prize that goes to those who "get it right first." Early movers can capture mind share and establish standards when the field is still uncrowded; they can block followers through patents and pre-emptive acquisition of scarce resources; they learn from their production experience, optimizing processes to decrease costs while increasing quality; and they benefit from switching costs when shifting vendors requires customers to retry and retrain on an innovation.

But because early movers, by definition, pioneer new market space, they are exposed to greater uncertainties than laggards. There is no prize for those who get it wrong first. While early movers flail about trying to find the right product architecture to position in the right market segment, it is the latecomers that reap the benefits of pioneering failures. And so, losing exemplars—Ampex in video recorders, Raytheon in microwave ovens, Chux in disposable diapers, and MITS in personal computers—are held up as proof that pioneers are the ones with arrows in their backs.

These dueling lists of examples and counterexamples make one thing clear: the relevant question for managers is not whether early movers *can* be advantaged but, rather, under what conditions they *will* be advantaged. We can better understand the relationship between entry timing and advantage by using the *First-mover Matrix* opposite.

The debate about first-mover advantage has hinged on the likelihood that the early mover enters the market with the right

		COMPLEMENTOR CO-INNOVATION CHALLENGE	
		LOWER	HIGHER
INNOVATOR EXECUTION CHALLENGE	LOWER	*Quadrant 1: First in Gets the Win* • Baseline level of early-mover advantage	*Quadrant 3: Hurry Up and Wait* • Reduced level of early-mover advantage
	HIGHER	*Quadrant 2: Winner Takes More* • Increased level of early-mover advantage	*Quadrant 4: It Depends* • Level of early-mover advantage depends on which challenge is resolved first.

Fig. 6.1: First-mover matrix for determining relative advantage from early entry as a function of the level of innovator execution challenge and complementor co-innovation challenge. *(Adapted from Adner and Kapoor, 2010.)*

product. In our terminology, the focus has been on execution. And the expected size of the advantage is directly linked to the size of the execution challenge: being first to market with an easy-to-implement, and hence imitate, product (a new office chair design or a vitamin-enhanced beverage) will yield a lesser prize than pioneering a harder-to-implement product (a new engine design or a supercomputer). In a product world, this makes sense.

This is the logic behind quadrants 1 and 2 in the first-mover matrix. Quadrant 1 (first in gets the win) is the baseline level of early-mover advantage—how big a win we can expect the early mover to enjoy. The greater the execution challenge you need to overcome to deliver the product, the harder it is for followers to ride on your coattails, and the bigger the reward for being early. This is the situation in quadrant 2 (winner takes more).

In a product-based world, this makes sense. But in an ecosystem world, this logic is incomplete. In an ecosystem world, as we have seen time and again, delivering a brilliant product that the competition cannot match is not enough. We need to make sure that all the other elements that our product requires to create its value are in place as well. When the co-innovation challenges in the ecosystem are high, this leads to the "hurry up and wait" syndrome of quadrant 3. Recall Nokia in 3G, Sony in e-books, and SaeHan in MP3 players: all raced to launch a great product into the market, and all fell flat. Why? Because being first doesn't matter if the critical complements aren't in place.

Over time, as firms and partners work through their challenges, the natural tendency of the ecosystem is to drift toward the upper left segment of the matrix. When execution and co-innovation challenges are both high at the time of entry (quadrant 4), the advantage of the entrant will depend on which challenge is resolved first—whether the system shifts to quadrant 2 (better) or quadrant 3 (worse).

The First-Mover Matrix at Work

How big a deal is this really? And can we actually get guidance from this approach? To answer these questions, I undertook a four-year project focused on the semiconductor lithography industry with Rahul Kapoor, my coauthor on the research studies. We used an ecosystem lens to explore early-mover advantage during the introduction of nine different technology generations between 1962 and 2005. The results, and their implications, are striking.

Semiconductor lithography is the beating heart of the digital revolution, the principle technology that has powered the improvements predicted by Moore's law (the prediction that the number of transistors that can be placed on a chip will double approximately every two years). It is the process by which circuit designs are imprinted on a semiconductor wafer—the process that allowed

Intel to fit 3 million transistors on a Pentium chip in 1993 and now, thanks to the improvements we will explore, 2.8 billion transistors on a Xeon chip in 2011.

Semiconductor lithography is a replication process that, in simplified terms, is a lot like old-fashioned chemical photography. At its core is the lithography *tool* (the camera body) into which are integrated two critical components: an *energy source* (flash) and a *lens* system (lens). For a lithography tool to create value, however, it must be used in conjunction with two key complements: a circuit *mask*, which holds the circuit design that is to be replicated (the object to be photographed), and a *resist* (chemical developer) that will react when exposed to the energy source to replicate the circuit image on the mask onto the silicon wafer (the photo paper).

Throughout its history, the driving goal of semiconductor lithography has been to increase image resolution (this is because resolution determines the extent of miniaturization and circuit density that can be achieved by a semiconductor manufacturer in its microchips). In the 1960s, resolution was in the range of 7,000 nanometers (0.007 mm). In 2011, it is 22 nanometers—a 300-fold performance improvement. Underlying this phenomenal pace of improvement have been a series of technology revolutions in the design of the tool as well as in the elements that are brought together in the lithography process. But despite all the changes to the different elements, the basic structure of the lithography ecosystem has not changed in over fifty years: the lens and the energy source are essential components that are integrated into the tool by the toolmaker (firms like Canon, Nikon, and ASML), while the mask and the resist are critical complements that are brought together by the customer (semiconductor manufacturers like Samsung, Toshiba, and Intel).

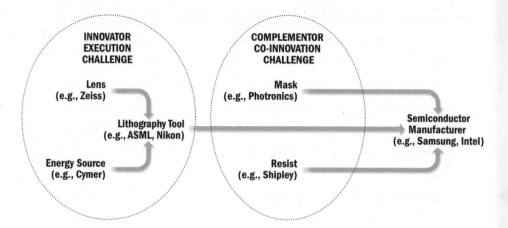

Figure 6.2: The semiconductor lithography equipment ecosystem. *(Adapted from Adner and Kapoor, 2010.)*

New generations of lithography tools are marked by transitions to more sophisticated architectures that provide greater control and repeatability, shifting from mechanical to electromechanical to electronic controls; from reflective to refractive light management; and incorporating digital logic throughout the device. What is interesting is that the innovation challenges at different points in the ecosystem varied quite dramatically across the different generations. Sometimes, the lens technology used in one generation could simply be reused in the next. At other times, entirely new lens materials and manufacturing processes would need to be developed to pass a new wavelength of light. In some generations, the energy source could simply be replicated, while in others, new categories of lasers needed to be invented. Similarly, some generations required major innovations in mask and resist while others did not. Thus, across the different generations, depending on how many different elements needed to be innovated and how great a change each required, we can characterize a range of co-innovation challenges that feed into the firm's ability to deliver its own innovation (the extent of execution innovation challenges) and co-innovation challenges that affect the ability to deliver the full value proposition to the end consumer (the extent of complementor co-innovation challenges).

It is the combination of this variance in the levels of execution and co-innovation challenges in conjuction with the stable ecosystem structure that allows us to compare outcomes across the nine technology generations and draw conclusions about the industry.

When Do Early Movers Win?

The tool manufacturers and their partners have a deeply held belief in the power of first-mover advantage. And the classic product-based indicators all suggest it should be high: there is a lot of coordination with customers and industry organizations like SEMATECH about the desired technical specifications of new technology generations, so uncertainty about requirements of the "right" product is low. Early movers gain significant learning curve advantages, reducing their costs and increasing their quality with rising production volumes. And, most important, because the semiconductor manufacturers customize their production techniques to the specific tool they buy, there are high costs to switching tool suppliers: once a customer adopts your tool, they are very unlikely to switch to a rival.

But when we applied an ecosystem lens in conjunction with statistical tools to isolate the relationship between how early firms entered and how much of a market share advantage they enjoyed, we identified a key contingency. In generations where complementor co-innovation challenges were low, the traditional product-based logic held true. In the baseline case of relatively low execution challenges (quadrant 1) early movers enjoyed a distinct advantage: a pioneer with a three-year head start could expect 3 percent higher market share advantage over the latecomer in total sales over the life of the generation. Keeping in mind that, in 2009, a 1 percent market share advantage in the new lithography tool generation (DUV 193i) equated to $28.4 million in annual sales, and that tool generations continue to be sold for many years, it is clear that the stakes are high. And it is assuring to see that the industry belief in first-mover advantage is fully supported in the baseline scenario.

When execution challenge is high and co-innovation challenge is low (quadrant 2), early movers are at an even greater advantage: a three-year head start yields a 6 percent market share advantage to the pioneer. Here, the belief in first-mover advantage is on even sounder footing.

The most intriguing finding, however, is the one that corresponds to the low execution challenge/high complementor co-innovation challenge scenario of quadrant 3. Here, the product-based logic breaks down in the face of ecosystem dynamics. Here, the first firm to overcome its execution challenge needs to wait. Here, the value proposition remains incomplete until all the complementors solve their problems as well. Here, the pioneer has no advantage. In fact, the pioneer is at a slight (−0.3 percent) market share disadvantage relative to laggards.

The implications of these findings are powerful. What they reveal is that it is fundamentally wrong to think about first-mover advantage as a fixed characteristic of an industry—any industry, including your own. Instead, we see that the extent of first-mover advantage depends on the nature of challenges in the ecosystem.

When development efforts are accelerated, costs rise exponentially. Whether or not they win a prize, a certainty for firms that race to be first is that they will pay a higher price for the attempt. Wise innovators will locate the nature of their endeavor on the first-mover matrix and adjust their speed accordingly. Aggressively pursuing first-mover advantage makes most sense when the innovator's execution challenges are high. This is the occasion for greater efforts because this is the time of greater rewards. It also shows that when complementors' co-innovation challenges are high, the rewards for pioneering are low. This is the occasion for watchful patience; the time for active preparation, but not for aggressive launch.

Smart-Mover Advantage

If you allow yourself to look beyond your own innovation challenges at the entirety of the value proposition, timing clues abound. It shouldn't take a visionary to see that demand for MP3 players won't take off until users have easy access to the actual product. It doesn't take a crystal ball to foretell that sales of a new lithography tool generation will flounder until the key complements are ready. And it doesn't take a lot of effort to figure out whether co-innovation challenges for a new innovation are high or low: in the semiconductor lithography industry we found articles discussing details of co-innovation challenges that were published as long as six years *before* the technology was commercialized.

Nevertheless, it does take willpower to resist the natural urge to rush forward. Self-imposed delays go against the grain of most leaders and organizations. But in an ecosystem world, the costly risk of "hurry up and wait" is a call for discipline and perspective. The ecosystem is a puzzle that needs to be assembled. The prize does not go to the first player to put down the first piece—because nothing happens until the puzzle is complete. The prize is only awarded after someone puts down the *last* piece.

Steve Jobs's iPod journey is an exemplary illustration. Jobs had the perspective to realize that digital music players were in a different quadrant than portable cassette players. The Walkman started life in quadrant 1. The MPMan started life in quadrant 3. Jobs understood that the natural trajectory of challenges is toward the upper left of the first-mover matrix. The "system" works to resolve co-innovation challenges, while industry rivals figure out execution. His insight was to "surf" the co-innovation wave, knowing that its challenges would be resolved over time. His brilliance was to wait to expend his energy on the execution challenge.

Jobs waited, but while he waited, he also differentiated. Apple didn't launch the iPod as a product. In combination with its iTunes music management software, the iPod was a solution. As the iPod's co-innovation risks faded away in 2001, Jobs launched. With his proprietary hardware-software combination, he didn't just put down the last piece, he put down the last two pieces. And he made sure they interlocked. By shifting to offering solutions, Apple increased the execution challenge for itself as well as for everyone else, effectively lowering the value of competitors' previous efforts and increasing the barrier for rivals to achieve future success. In doing so, he thrust the iPod into quadrant 2, to capture smart-mover advantage. (In chapter 8 we will see Jobs deploy a variant of this strategy with the iPhone and the iPad tablet.)

Smart timing—for a novel product or an entirely new technology—requires a sober look at who and what else is out there to help or hinder the effort. Understanding these dynamics informs decision makers, helping you dial up or dial down your level of aggression going forward. As ecosystems become ever more pervasive, it is critical to ask the question: "Are we in a Walkman world or in an iPod world?" As you choose your moment to strike, looking around at both the structure of the ecosystem and your role in it, you are now in a better position to win. There's still uncertainty, of course. No triumph is preordained. But understanding your effort from an ecosystem perspective stacks the odds in your favor. The blinders are off. Welcome to the bigger picture.

■ ■ ■

EXPANDING THE PERSPECTIVE MEANS CHANGING THE CONVERSATION

Choosing to participate in an ecosystem means needing to make a multitude of new choices regarding roles, positioning, and timing. The wide-lens tools and frameworks developed in this book will be of help in structuring these decisions.

The wise manager, however, knows that management frameworks, in general, and strategy frameworks, in particular, should be approached with care. When confronted with a decision or an opportunity, we often start with an intuition about what the right course of action is. Judicious, unbiased application of a framework can change this intuition. But as anyone who has spent time in meetings will know, unbiased application is not always the rule.

In my opinion, the greatest value of strategy frameworks lies in clarifying the issues that arise when different managers with different starting intuitions disagree over the right course of action. In a group setting, frameworks are tools for communication and debate. Used correctly, a good framework shifts the interaction from a battle of guts—too often resolved on the basis of reputation, power, and eloquence—to an organized comparison of the assumptions being made about a given situation's fundamental structure. Surfacing these differences in hidden assumptions is often the key to finding effective solutions.

My hope is that the tools and frameworks developed in this book, by providing a clear grammar for discussing the structure of interdependence and its implications for your success, will make your debates more productive and their resolutions more robust.

Put another way: while using these tools will be of value to the lone analyst, it will be of greater value to the project team, and of greatest value to a consortium of partners. This will also be the case in part 3, as we shift from choice to intervention. I will introduce new strategies for building and shaping ecosystems—how to reconfigure the structure of dependence and how to leverage advantage within and across ecosystems. I will show how the wide-lens toolbox can be credibly deployed to avoid needless failures and multiply your odds of success.

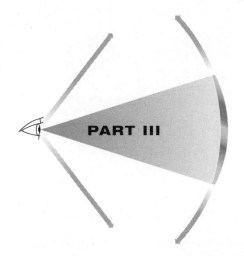

PART III

Winning the Game

III. Winning the Game

II. Choosing Your Position

I. Seeing the Ecosystem

Chapter 9
Multiplying
Your Odds
of Success

Chapter 8
Sequencing
Success

Chapter 7
Changing
the Game

Main Cases:
Electric Car   M-PESA
and Better   and
Place   Apple

Tools:
5 Levers   MVF,
                     Staged Expansion,
                     Carryover

Changing the Game:

Reconfiguring the Ecosystem to Work for You

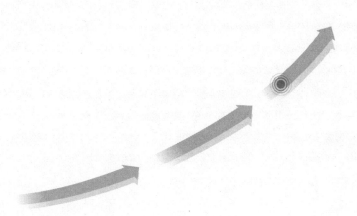

Every success story that we have encountered so far shares a common characteristic: each innovator, having taken a hard look at the ecosystem, found a way to eliminate all the red lights from his value blueprint before moving forward.

What is more intriguing is that these innovators also shared a common *path* to success. For digital cinema, Amazon's Kindle, and Apple's iPod, the shift from red to green was not just a matter of working harder, or of incentivizing and cajoling partners to ensure that each piece of the ecosystem puzzle fell into place.

Rather, in each case, success came from first recognizing the key constraints that held back value creation and then taking bold steps to reconfigure the blueprint to work around those constraints.

Innovating in ecosystems demands not just innovation in the discrete elements but also innovation in the way in which the elements come together—innovation in the blueprint itself. The Hollywood studios added new elements into their ecosystem—the virtual print fee mechanism and the third-party integrator—that allowed them to share their benefits with the movie theater owners who were so critical to the success of the plan. Amazon bundled the previously separate elements of the e-book reader with an electronic bookstore and used ecosystem partners to relocate the task of connectivity from the consumer to the Kindle device. Apple combined hardware with music management software and then added the new element of simple, secure online music purchase.

This chapter is about how to change the structure of the ecosystem to work for you. We will identify the *Five Levers of Ecosystem Reconfiguration* and explore how they can be used to modify your value blueprint to eliminate the adoption and co-innovation bottlenecks to your value creation.

We will examine the case of the electric car, a transportation solution that has excited consumers, firms, and governments alike with its promise of energy independence, cleaner air, green jobs, and lower fuel costs. This will not be an analysis of a past example whose outcomes are already known; rather, we will be exploring a still-unfolding case that is being actively shaped as I write this book. We will start by identifying the major challenges in the current ecosystem—three that are clearly visible and three that are revealed when we use a wide lens. These are the red lights stopping electric vehicles (EVs) from breaking into the mainstream consumer market.

Seeing the bigger picture almost always exposes bigger problems. But it also gives rise to the possibility of finding more robust solutions. To this end, we will consider the approach being pursued by a promising EV start-up company, Better Place. Because the outcomes are not yet known, the analysis will be prospective. But we will find the company's strategy highly instructive for the way in which it deploys a combination of all five reconfiguration levers to create a pathway to success.

The Early Days of the Electric Car

The electric car is an old proposition. At the turn of the twentieth century, the future of the automobile industry was anybody's game as electric-, gas-, and steam-powered cars all vied for technological supremacy. In fact, the American Electric Vehicle Company, headed by financier William C. Whitney, was, at its height in 1899,

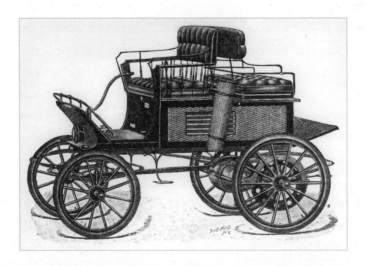

Figure 7.1: An American Electric Vehicle Company electric car from 1900. (© Top Foto / The Image Works.)

the largest car manufacturer in the United States. The electric car was clean and quiet, compared to the more complex, loud and dirty gas-powered automobile. An 1897 editorial captured the sentiment when professing, "There is every reason to believe that the electric vehicle industry is well established on a sure foundation and that it will grow rapidly."

But by the early 1900s, confronted by efficiency improvements in gasoline engines, the discovery of cheap oil in Texas, and Henry Ford's mass-manufacturing triumph of the Model T, the electric vehicle had definitively lost the race. In 1914, there were 568,000 automobiles manufactured in the United States; 99 percent of these contained gasoline-burning internal combustion engines.

It wasn't until the 1990s that the electric car enjoyed a small renaissance due to a combination of technology improvements and government mandates. This rebirth was centered in California— the largest car market in the United States—and home to both wealthy environmentally conscious consumers and aggressive state government policy makers. The effort began in 1990 with GM's unveiling of the Impact, an all-electric concept car, at the Los Angeles Auto Show. The Impact was a catalyst for the California Air Resources Board (CARB) Zero Emission Vehicle (ZEV) Program, which mandated that, by 1998, 2 percent of vehicles produced for sale in California had to be zero-emission vehicles, increasing to 5 percent in 2001 and 10 percent in 2003. In response to CARB's mandate, GM introduced the EV1, the world's first commercially available all-electric vehicle. Other big automotive players soon joined in with their own all-electric offerings, including Nissan's Altra EV, Honda's EV Plus, and Toyota's RAV4 EV. But all these programs were scrapped in the early 2000s due to a combination of legal challenges to the CARB mandate and unattractive consumer economics that stemmed from high leasing costs (the monthly lease rate for the EV1, a two-passenger subcompact coupe, was between $399 and $549 per month—comparable to a luxury sedan), constrained driving ranges, and limited charging infrastructure.

Today, we are witnessing the third wave in the attempted emergence of the electric car. And now the promise of the proposition is more urgent than ever. Greenhouse gas emissions are an important contributor to global warming. With approximately 1 billion vehicles already on the world's roads churning out emissions, and rapid growth forecast for new economies, there is a pressing need for an alternative to gasoline. Beyond environmental cost, is the economic cost. The United States, for example, imported 61 percent of its oil in 2010, over 4 billion barrels. At the prevailing price of the time—$76 per barrel—this amounted to a transfer of $325 billion to foreign governments, or $619,225 per minute. With demand for oil increasing with the rise of new economies, and questions about the availability of future reserves, there is a general consensus that future prices are likely to be higher, and substantially so.

To date, the story of the electric car has been one of technology visionaries and environmental diehards. Yes, there is a small, but very visible, consumer segment for whom the benefit of saving the planet and/or showing off green credentials is worth the premium. But for the electric car to make an impact on energy independence and pollution, it must move beyond this niche market and appeal to mainstream buyers. How?

Challenges in the Electric Vehicle Ecosystem

From the start, the electric vehicle (EV) has been perceived as an ecosystem problem, in which multiple elements need to come together to enable the value proposition (see figure 7.2).

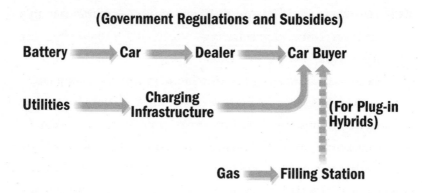

Figure 7.2: Value blueprint of the electric vehicle (EV) ecosystem including gasoline supply for plug-in hybrid.

Three clearly visible hurdles to the mass adoption of the EV proposition have garnered the attention of the media, policy makers, and entrepreneurs across the globe. First, electric vehicles are more expensive to purchase than comparable gas-powered cars. Second, the distance one can drive before exhausting the charge in the battery is inferior to that of gas-powered cars. Third, the infrastructure for recharging batteries in terms of both the availability of charge spots as well as the time required for charging, is vastly inferior to the infrastructure already in place for gas-powered cars. Interestingly, these are the same challenges that confronted the electric car back in 1908.

Problem A: Purchase Price Premium

The economic argument for buying an EV is based on the fact that electric miles are much cheaper than gasoline miles. At $4 per gallon and 25 miles per gallon, the cost of every gasoline mile is $0.16. In contrast, with electricity priced at $0.12 per kilowatt hour (kWh) and 4 miles per kWh, the cost of every electric mile is

$0.03. Driving an EV is like getting your gasoline at $0.75 per gallon. This is certainly appealing.

However, while driving an EV may be cheap, actually buying one is not. Compare the new Nissan Leaf, launched in 2011 with a retail price of $33,000 (not including the $2,000 home charger installation fee), to the similarly sized Nissan Versa, which lists for $13,500. At the heart of this price difference is the cost of the Leaf's 24 kWh battery, estimated at $15,600 for the early versions of the car. With the current $7,500 federal tax incentive for all EV purchases, that's still a $12,000 difference. And $12,000 buys a lot of gas. Assuming you do save 13 cents on every mile you drive, in this scenario you'll have to travel over 75,000 miles just to break even.

Problem B: Limited Driving Range

"Range anxiety" is the official industry term for the fear of running out of power mid-journey in an EV. As a representative EV, a fully charged Leaf can go approximately 100 miles before draining its battery, while the comparable gas-powered Versa can travel over 400 miles on a full tank of gas. Live in hilly terrain? Carrying a heavy load? Running the air conditioner? All these elements must be taken into consideration while planning a simple trip. Most drives are well within this range, but there is a lot of variance. Even if you take a 200-mile trip only once a month, the range limit would preclude the EV from becoming a complete driving solution.

An EV's range limit is primarily determined by its battery. One approach to solving the range problem is to develop a better battery, and billions of dollars have been dedicated to this goal. While there is no doubt that these improvements will come about eventually, there is great uncertainty about how many years will pass before they will be achieved. A big question is how everyone else in the system is to sustain and motivate their own efforts while they wait.*

Problem C: Charging Infrastructure

Related to the question of driving range is the question of battery charging. Here, there are two hurdles: the availability of charge spots and the time it takes to charge. According to the U.S. Department of Energy's National Renewable Energy Laboratory, there were 3,834 public charge stations deployed across 39 states as of September 30, 2011 (1,202 of which were in California). Compare this to 159,006 gasoline service stations, the vast majority of which have multiple pumps, and then assess convenience. EV drivers have little choice but to recharge their cars at home. But regardless of whether they recharge their batteries at home or in a public spot, fully recharging a spent battery takes time: eight hours with a 220-volt charger, twenty hours with a 110-volt charger. Level 3 chargers, which run at 500 volts, can recharge a battery in thirty minutes. But because they are far more expensive, and also have the potential to degrade the battery's lifetime performance, they constitute only a tiny minority of installations. On a long trip, recharging the battery is a meaningful interruption to travel. Compared with the option of a five-minute fillup at the local gas station, the EV proposition again falls short for most drivers.

Charging infrastructure, of course, has all the classic characteristics of a chicken-and-egg problem: the private incentive to

---

* An alternative approach is to use current battery technology, just more of it. Tesla's Roadster made headlines in 2009 when it became the first commercially available EV with a range of almost 250 miles—competitive with gasoline cars. Tesla doubled the driving range by doubling the number of battery cells. However, this also doubled the price: the Roadster battery alone costs an estimated $36,000 (the base MSRP for the 2011 Roadster is $109,000), undermining its economic attractiveness to the mainstream.

invest in infrastructure is low until there are enough EVs on the road, while the appeal of EVs remains stunted until there is an extensive charging infrastructure already deployed.

In the United States, the Department of Energy has allocated $400 million to EV infrastructure and is working with several private companies to install and manage the charge spots. A concern here, however, is that, because these are taxpayer funds, the deployment is disbursed across a vast number of cities and regions along politically influenced lines. While each additional charge spot is a contribution, it is unclear whether the network is being built along the most efficient lines.

An innovative alternative has been the introduction of plug-in hybrids like GM's 2011 Chevy Volt, which combines a lithium-ion battery with an on-board gas-powered generator that engages only after the battery is depleted. The idea is to use the current gas station infrastructure to ease customer range anxiety while still enjoying the green benefits of an EV.

Drivers reaching the end of their battery power can simply fuel up at a gas station and rely on their gas generators to take them to their destination. But, given the necessity of both an electric and gas engine, the Volt is an expensive proposition at $41,000—more than twice as much as the comparably sized, similarly equipped Chevrolet Cruze, which landed in dealerships in 2011 at a base price of $16,275. Once again, that premium could buy a lot gas. And once again, leveraging existing technology seems to undermine the economic attractiveness of the offer. The Volt, according to IHS Automotive analyst George Magliano, is a "statement vehicle" for GM. "But do I think it's going to be a volume seller? No." Which leads to the major critique, "How can we save the planet if [companies] are pitching these products only to the rich?"

Taken together, the adoption and co-innovation challenges embedded in these three problems (purchase price premium, driving range, and charging infrastructure) paint a bleak picture. But like most technology obstacles, they are addressable. And indeed, around the globe, governments and companies are investing tremendous effort, resources, and time to overcome these challenges.

Hidden Threats to the Electric Vehicle Value Proposition

Even if these first three problems were overcome, however, the electric car would remain a niche product. In order for the EV to make sense for the mainstream consumer, there are three additional hurdles that must also be cleared, challenges that are currently lurking in the blind spot of many of the organizations that are investing enormous amounts of money and talent in the EV effort.

Problem D: Battery Resale Value

As already discussed under problem A (Purchase Price Premium), battery costs constrain the economic viability of EVs. But there is an even bigger battery-related problem than the acquisition price of the electric car: the impact of the battery on the resale value of the car.

Thanks to substantial investment by both the public and private sectors, battery technology is constantly and rapidly improving, generation after generation. Battery performance (measured by ability to hold more energy in less space, temperature robustness, and production costs) is improving at a much faster rate than any other component of the car. Forecasts vary widely, but by some estimates the cost per kWh may drop from approximately $650 in 2011 to $350 by 2015. A 24 kWh battery would then cost $8,400 instead of $15,600.

This is great news—but only for those who don't already own an EV. The battery is the most expensive part of an electric vehicle, and it is also the part that becomes obsolete the fastest.

Moreover, batteries have limited lives, measured in terms of the number of charging cycles they can sustain before their performance (ability to hold the charge) degrades below a reasonable level. According to Kiplinger, a key component of a new car's value and attractiveness for a consumer is what it will be worth after three to five years of use. The estimated $15,600 battery in a 2011 EV has a range of a hundred miles. If by 2015 you can have an EV with a brand-new battery, presumably with greater range and longer cycle life, for $8,400, then how much would you be willing to pay for a used four-year-old EV? The inevitable battery improvements mean a four-year-old EV will be a relic. Suddenly, the calculation of an EV's resale value starts to look more like reselling a used computer than a used car. *Red light.*

Problem E: Limited Driving Range Limits Savings

Limited driving range erodes not just the convenience but also the economic benefits of the electric car. EV enthusiasts hold to this incontrovertible fact: the real savings from purchasing an electric car comes from avoiding the gas pump. With every mile you drive, you save! But this matters only if you are traveling great distances. The reality of a limited charging infrastructure means that, for most adopters, the EV will be the "city car" that they drive to work and for local errands. But in limiting their driving range to short distances, the city car usage case also limits the potential for economic advantage. This is a big problem: yes, the more you drive, the more you save; but as long as the range of your EV is limited, so too will be the range of your savings. *Red light.*

Problem F: Electric Grid Capacity

Imagine that all the concerns raised above have been addressed. The policy makers have succeeded in prodding the different actors into action; the myriad car manufacturers have found a way to sell EVs at a price that competes with gas-fueled competitors; the battery makers have extended their driving range; and communities and infrastructure firms have cooperated to blanket the country in a dense web of charge spots. As mass-market buyers finally embrace the EV proposition, is success finally at hand?

No. The failure of the traditional electric car is embedded within its path to success. Car usage is as predictable as commuter rush hours. Approximately 90 percent of driving occurs as part of our daily commute as we drive from home to work and back again. This means that, since most of us are driving at the same time of day, we're also *not* driving at the same times of day. And this means that the majority of EV drivers will plug in their EVs around 8:30 or 9:00 a.m. when arriving at work and then again in the early evening when returning home. As long as just a handful of drivers adopt EVs, this is not a problem (but remember: if it is relegated to just a handful of drivers, the EV is not a solution to oil dependence, environmental damage, and high fuel costs). What would happen if a substantial percentage of drivers adopted EVs?

There are over 5 million registered cars in Los Angeles County alone. If just 5 percent were electric (250,000 vehicles would be a great success, though still not nearly enough to make a meaningful dent in the environmental quality or the economics of oil imports), plugging them in to recharge simultaneously would place a 750-megawatt load on the electric grid, equivalent to the generating capacity of two midsize power plants. Having EV penetration of 25 percent would impose a 3,750-gigawatt load, which is over a third of L.A. County's average electric load! If the EV was adopted by the mass of consumers, and everyone in a community were to plug in at the same time, the sudden surge in power demand would send a shock wave through the electric grid that could overwhelm the distribution and generation networks, causing a power blackout.

To be sure, achieving even 5 percent market adoption will take some time—forever, if the other red lights aren't successfully addressed. But this final point highlights the need for a scalable solution to be in place on the power generation/distribution side of the ecosystem if successfully turning all those other red lights to green is to have a chance at enabling mass adoption. Thus, the final hurdle for the electric car could be electricity itself.

Paradoxically, as long as the electric car fails to break into the mainstream, the challenge of the electric grid can be ignored. But once it does succeed in attracting mainstream buyers, the inability of the grid to support demand will drive its failure. In contrast to the usual problems of emergence that we have examined, the problem here is one of scalability: the light is green as long as there is no traffic; but once traffic picks up, we have a flashing red light on our blueprint.

The good news here is that around the world governments and utilities are investing to deploy smart-grid technologies to help circumvent this problem. "Smart grid" is a catchall term for a host of technologies that can respond to, and even predict, the individual demands placed on the electric system and adjust load and distribution accordingly. These include smart meters that adjust the price charged for electricity in real time, smart automation that can turn electric equipment and appliances on or off depending on the load on the grid, and smart distribution that can help ensure that local power lines are not overloaded. The better news is that this technology is already available. But the harsh reality is that it is expensive to acquire and time intensive to deploy. The smart grid is coming but on its own schedule. Whether it will be ready in time for the mass adoption of electric vehicles is an open question.

Individual Execution vs. System Viability

Looking at the EV proposition through a wide lens reveals a list of challenges that goes far beyond simply building an electric car that goes the distance. The core hurdles have to do with the general problems surrounding electricity: generating it, storing it, delivering it, and—for drivers—paying for it. Until these concerns are successfully addressed, the sad history of the electric car will continue to repeat itself.

The broad array of players—public and private—that are devoting substantial resources to solving the EV dilemma along the traditional lines are focusing on their own narrow execution challenges while hoping that the system will somehow "find" a way of coming together. But while these efforts are improving the quality of every individual element of the system, there is a great deal of incoherence in the way that the system is developing as a collective. From the perspective of any given actor, the path to success is blocked by unresolved co-innovation risk and adoption chain risk. We've seen this before. Hope is not a strategy. Without leadership, the system could converge, but it is unlikely to converge along a path that is either timely or efficient. Is there a better way?

The Five Levers of Ecosystem Reconfiguration

Solving ecosystem problems requires an ecosystem approach: taking the existing pieces and finding a way to reconfigure the puzzle. We saw this approach used in chapter 3, as the Hollywood studios reconfigured the digital cinema blueprint, and again in chapter 4, as Amazon reconfigured the e-book blueprint. In both cases, success did not come from discrete technology improvements. And it did not come from vertical integration—bringing external activities inside the firm. Neither better technologies nor increased control were sufficient to unblock the bottlenecks to value creation. Instead, success came from accepting the limitations of the existing elements and then finding a new way to bring them together.

Reconfiguring an ecosystem entails changing the pattern of interaction among the elements in the system. Taking any value blueprint as a starting point and looking at the arrangement of activities, actors, and links, we can ask five fundamental questions to uncover a new configuration that can eliminate the problematic bottlenecks:

1. What can be *separated*?

    Is there an opportunity to decouple elements that are currently bundled in a way that can create new value and move the value proposition forward?

2. What can be *combined*?

    Is there an opportunity to bundle elements that are currently uncoupled in a way that can create new value and move the value proposition forward?

3. What can be *relocated*?

    Is there an opportunity to shift existing elements to new positions in the ecosystem in a way that can create new value and move the value proposition forward?

4. What can be *added*?

    Are there elements that are currently absent but whose introduction to the ecosystem can create new value and move the value proposition forward?

5. What can be *subtracted*?

Are there existing elements whose elimination from the ecosystem could be accommodated in a way that would allow for the creation of new value and move the value proposition forward?

These questions are not simply about change. Recall that Sony *added* its own proprietary bookstore to its e-book initiative—to little avail. Sony failed to see the rest of the problem: that without a convenient way for consumers to have access to a lot of content, the market could not take off. Compare this to Amazon's effort: the company did spot the real hurdle and asked itself: what can we combine? By incorporating a wireless link between the Kindle device to its already popular store, Amazon enabled users to effortlessly access content in seconds. And with this blueprint

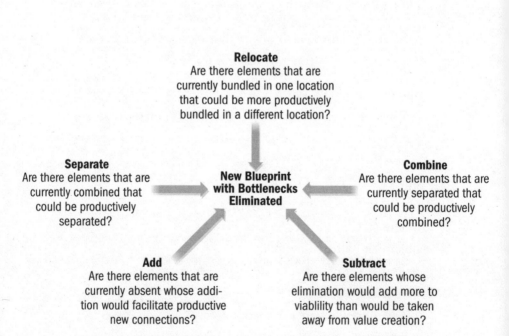

Figure 7.3: The five levers of ecosystem reconfiguration.

clearly in mind, the company shifted its position from device maker to ecosystem leader, enticing publishers and customers to embrace the value proposition.

Recall the red light that held back the promise of digital cinema. Theater owners could not see the relative benefit of going digital when the outlay was so high. Once they recognized this problem, the movie studios—for whom going digital promised tremendous cost savings—stepped in and asked a key question: what can we add? The digital cinema integrator and the virtual print fee link were added to the blueprint to enable a financing model that subsidized the exhibitors and moved digital cinema into the mainstream.

We witnessed a similar ecosystem reconfiguration in chapter 6. As various MP3 players vied for dominance, Apple made its move, asking, what can be combined? An elegant device merged with smart software meant that a key problem to the portable MP3 player proposition was solved: users now had an intuitive way to manage their music collection. Then, by adding the iTunes Music Store, Apple cemented its win.

Employing the levers, alone or in combination, can be helpful in revealing the path to a viable solution. Now consider the six EV problems:

Problem A: Purchase Price Premium
Problem B: Limited Driving Range
Problem C: Charging Infrastructure
Problem D: Battery Resale Value
Problem E: Limited Driving Range Limits Savings
Problem F: Electric Grid Capacity

How might reconfiguring the ecosystem help address each of these problems and unlock the EV value proposition?

Just such an approach to solving the EV problem—one that considers the ecosystem holistically rather than each piece individually—is being pursued by a fascinating new company named Better Place. At the time of this writing, Better Place is on the verge of its first commercial deployment: the company is planning a market launch in Israel for early 2012, followed by a launch in Denmark later that year, with additional countries and regions to come.

While Better Place's outcomes are yet to be determined, the start-up's approach offers an object lesson in how to think about ecosystem strategy.

Better Place: A Different Approach to EVs

Better Place was founded in 2007 by Shai Agassi, who turned down the opportunity to become CEO of software giant SAP in order to pursue an innovative vision for gasoline-free cars. "I'd rather fail at Better Place than succeed at SAP because no other job could compare to trying to save the world," he explained. His strategy is as bold as his decision.

Better Place is attempting to reconfigure the EV ecosystem. Its strategy starts by embracing the problems we raised above as constraints on its blueprint design. The company's starting premises are that:

- For economic attractiveness, consumers should not own the battery (problems A and D).
- For both functional and economic attractiveness, range and convenience cannot be limited (problems B, C, and E).
- For scalable success, the existing electric grid cannot be disturbed (problem F).

- And for business viability, a solution must be found using currently available technology, rather than wait for future miracles.

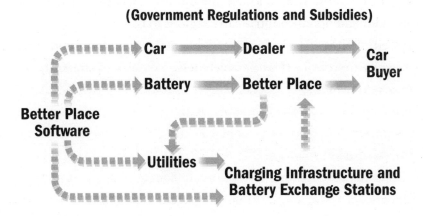

Figure 7.4: The Better Place value blueprint.

The New Proposition for Consumers

Better Place's approach is not to innovate the electric car but rather to innovate the ecosystem *around* the car. By reconfiguring this system, Better Place changes the nature of the value proposition for almost every actor in it, starting with the car buyer.

In this blueprint, the car and the battery are separated. Rather than buying a car that includes a battery, the driver purchases and owns the car, while Better Place purchases and owns the battery. In exchange for a mileage-based monthly fee, the company installs charge spots in the driver's home and workplace, gives the driver use of the battery, offers free access to the charging infrastructure that Better Place itself builds out, and includes all the electricity required for battery charging. It also offers unlimited battery exchanges.

As a package, this solves the core problems that undermine the traditional EV value proposition for consumers. By excluding the battery from the car purchase (in the same way that gasoline is excluded from a traditional car purchase), the EV can be offered at a competitive price. For example, in the United States the acquisition cost of the Leaf without a battery would be $33,000 (retail price) minus $15,600 (cost of battery), for a total of $17,400. After applying the $7,500 government rebate for electric cars, you could potentially purchase a brand-new EV for less than $10,000! Problem A solved.

And because Better Place owns the battery, the question of its obsolescence and resale value disappears—at least for the consumer. As a for-profit company, Better Place is in a much better position to handle obsolescence because it can depreciate the value of the battery against company profits. Moreover, when the fully depreciated battery can no longer hold sufficient charge for automotive use, it can be resold to utility and industrial markets as a cheap power storage and power backup solution. Problem D solved.

By providing a home charging spot and proactively building out the public charging infrastructure, Better Place addresses the availability side of charging convenience in problem C. Here, the advantage of a tight geographic boundary becomes clear: by the time of its Israel launch, Better Place will have installed thousands of charge spots throughout the country (population 7.5 million, area 8,019 square miles). Compare this with the 1,202 public charge spots deployed (as of September 30, 2011) throughout the most EV friendly state in the United States, California (population 37 million, area 158,706 square miles).

To help manage charging needs, EVs that work with the Better

Place network come equipped with an overarching software operating system, dubbed OScar. For the consumer, this onboard software is an interactive tool that anticipates the driver's energy needs depending on destination and time of day and locates available charges spots. It also connects to roadside assistance in case of emergencies and serves as a navigation aid. And because Better Place—an industrial bulk buyer that can shed load on demand, and hence be the beneficiary of extremely low electricity rates—purchases the electricity that comes even from your home charger, this translates into much lower electricity cost per mile. Problem C addressed, at least in part, as well as some headway on problem E.

The battery exchange station is the EV equivalent of an automated gas station, with the promise that a battery change will take less time than filling up a gas tank. In a setup that evokes an automated car-wash line, the driver pulls onto a conveyor system where a robotic arm removes the old battery from beneath the car and replaces it with a fully charged one, all in a matter of minutes. With the switch station, the range of an EV is thus no longer limited by the hundred-mile range of its battery, but by the density of the switch station network: as long as you can get to a switch station, you can go another hundred miles.

Better Place promises to deploy these stations at regular intervals along all major routes—four stations along every hundred-mile stretch, guaranteeing complete coverage of a geographic location and ensuring that a fully charged battery will always be available. In advance of its Israel launch, it has deployed twenty switch stations across the country, with forty planned by the end of the first year. Within the geography, the driving range issue (problem B) is solved, as is the challenge that the economic advantage of cheaper fuel cost per mile only comes with distance (problem E).

It is interesting to note that the idea of the battery switch station can work only if batteries are not owned by individual drivers. Otherwise, drivers would be concerned with the potential of trading *their* precious battery for an inferior one. This benefit flows directly from the reconfiguration of the ecosystem.

Creating the Win-Win-Win for Ecosystem Partners

While all of this enhances the Better Place offering for customers, one critical limitation arises. For a car to work with the system, it must be designed and built to interface with Better Place's service platform: battery bays that are compatible with the Better Place exchange station infrastructure, charging modules aligned with the charge spot standard to which Better Place has subscribed, and data interfaces compatible with Better Place's operating system. This means that auto manufacturers need to design cars specifically for the Better Place system.

Remember the run-flat failure?

The good news is that Better Place did too—and has managed this dependence proactively. In 2008, Better Place partnered with Renault to jointly commercialize a mass-market EV. This was possible because of CEO Carlos Ghosn's confidence in the future of electric cars (the Leaf is also his initiative through the Renault-Nissan Alliance). But a critical element was Agassi's willingness to commit to a scale that made it worthwhile for the carmaker to design the zero-emission Fluence Z.E. around Better Place specifications. Unlike other EV pilot projects, Better Place guaranteed volume: the company placed an order for 100,000 Fluence Z.E. cars back in 2009—four years before it had a single customer.

The implication, however, is that, at launch, customers who want to partake of the Better Place offer can drive only a Renault

Fluence Z.E. This is a real constraint but not necessarily a fatal flaw. Keep in mind Henry Ford's policy on variety for the Model T: "You can have any color you want, as long as it's black."

The New Proposition for Utilities

Because Better Place owns the battery, buys the electricity, manages the charging infrastructure, and runs the operating system inside the car, it has a rare view into the charging needs of any EV in its network and a unique ability to manage the charging process. These combine to allow the company to deal with utility power load head-on. By balancing power demand from cars with grid capacity, the solution enables utilities to sell more energy with no need to upgrade their infrastructure, while at the same time keeping the customer happy.

The Better Place software blankets the entire system, allowing the company to monitor the charge status of each battery—whether it's powering a car, plugged into a charge spot, or waiting at a switching station—and can anticipate when it will require more energy. It is also able to monitor the electric distribution network to know when it is approaching load capacity and when there is slack in the system. Using this information, Better Place can selectively charge different EVs on the system, delaying the power feed to those cars with batteries that are already quite full and which are going to be parked for a while, prioritizing charge to those cars whose batteries are low or whose drivers have signaled a desire for a full recharge. By exploiting the intelligence in the system and its visibility into the car, Better Place has provided a smart-grid solution for utilities without the need for utilities to deploy a smart grid.

Beyond intelligence in pulling power from the grid, the Better Place solution can use electricity stored in idle batteries to deliver power back to the grid when electricity demand threatens to exceed supply (for example, during peak hours on hot days when utilities are reaching their generation limits). While the idea of vehicle-to-grid (V2G) charging has been discussed for decades, two key obstacles stood in its way. First was the need for smart-grid technology that would allow for such signaling and two-way transfers. Second was the degradation in battery life that is caused by V2G charging. Despite the fact that utilities are willing to pay a big premium for kilowatts at times of peak load, expectations are that consumers will be unwilling to risk their investment in their battery. In the words of one potential buyer, "It's MY car, MY battery, and MY time. No, thanks, you can keep your pittance—not worth my inconvenience." Because Better Place owns the battery and has added intelligence into the charging network that it manages, both these constraints disappear. Problem F solved.

The Profit Proposition for Better Place

As deep-pocketed firms and governments around the world scramble to make the EV proposition a go, this new entrant has, at least on paper, solved all six of the EV constraints. How can Better Place afford such a radical proposition? While the vision seems radical in the context of cars, it is well established elsewhere. How can a mobile phone operator afford to "give" you a $300 phone for $50 while also deploying an infrastructure of base stations and antennas? The answer, as every cell phone user knows, is a multi-year service contract. Agassi's first insight was to find an analog in mobile operators, which subsidize the acquisition of the cell phone (battery), and then make money over the life of the contract in which the customer pays a subscription fee that includes a certain number of minutes (miles) each month.

But his second insight, no less crucial, was to identify the right target markets in which to deploy his novel proposition. Here, rather than setting his sights on the obvious prize of California and the U.S. market, Agassi fixated on markets whose structure would best offset his constraints of capital and existing technologies.

The profitability of the Better Place proposition hinges on the relative attractiveness of EVs over traditional gas-powered cars. This attractiveness depends on the combination of two elements: the relative price of electric miles compared to gasoline miles, and the relative price of electric cars compared to gasoline cars. (Note: A more detailed analysis appears in the endnotes.)

The first requirement is that the cost of electric miles (e-miles) is much cheaper than gasoline miles (g-miles). So much cheaper that Better Place can pay for the battery, pay for the electricity, pay for the infrastructure, capture a healthy margin for itself, and still be able to sell the miles to consumers at a price that roundly beats gasoline miles. This varies by country. In fact, other than in the United States, where the gasoline tax is far below the average of other Western countries (a realization that often surprises Americans), the gap between the cost of e-miles and g-miles is already substantial. In Denmark, where the average price of gasoline in July 2011 was $8.87 per gallon, and in Israel, where the price was $8.33, the price difference can be over $0.20 per mile. Driving 15,000 miles a year for four years amounts to a difference of $12,000. This disparity is expected to grow substantially as battery costs continue to decrease and gas prices rise.

The second determinant of attractiveness is the price of acquiring an EV compared to a gasoline car. This also varies by country. In Israel the purchase tax on conventional cars is 85 percent—nearly doubling the cost of the car before you drive it off the lot. But for electric cars the tax is a "mere" 10 percent (increasing to 30 percent in 2015). Denmark offers its citizens even greater motivation to go electric: conventional cars are taxed at 180 percent, EVs at 0 percent.

Denmark has a population of 5.5 million people and is one of the most environmentally conscious countries in the world—its EV tax exemption has been on the books for over a quarter of a century. Still, by 2010, there were fewer than 500 registered EVs in the entire country. Why? Because subsidies solve only the acquisition price issue (problem A). An EV that is less expensive but not functional is not a viable solution. If you are looking for a vehicle that is constrained to short-range travel, for most Danes the dominant choice is a bicycle.

But with the range constraint removed, the tax incentive gives Danish car buyers a viable choice: purchase a Fluence Z.E. at $37,962, with no added tax, or buy a comparable yet gas-powered car such as the Toyota Avensis, which has a pretax price of around $32,000, for up to $89,600, after tax. And while the 85 percent tax in Israel might now seem like a relative bargain, the tax exemption there similarly guarantees that buyers will see real, significant savings *up front*.

Limitations of the Approach

The Better Place offer will surely not appeal to everyone. The absence of initial choice in cars, the still unproven reliability of both the car and the network, the need for a dedicated parking location to allow for charging at home—these objections and others will limit the appeal of the proposition. The relevant question is not whether there will be customers who reject the offer but whether there will be enough customers who accept it. And a new car at 50 percent off is likely to hold at least a little appeal. One group for whom this offer seems especially attractive is corporate fleet managers who, in addition to appreciating lower acquisition prices, also regard the elimination of fuel price fluctuations for four years in their budgeting cycle as uniquely attractive. Indeed, this segment is a key focus for Better Place.

Better Place has harnessed a potent combination: focus *and* scale. Its novelty comes from its innovative approach to reconfiguring the ecosystem. But its effectiveness comes from combining this with an intelligent selection of target markets. It is precisely because the Israeli and Danish markets are so small—in terms of both geography and population—and so bounded that Better Place can afford to deploy a comprehensive infrastructure of charge spots and switch stations in advance of selling cars. These are ideal traffic islands in a way that Los Angeles County cannot be. And it is precisely because the tax regimes in these countries were so compelling that the company can find the confidence (and instill this confidence in the investors who have entrusted over $700 million to them before their launch) that its offer will be attractive to a meaningful number of buyers and, in turn, subsidize the participation of all the other players through purchase contracts that commit to both volumes and dates. This combination of focus and scale is the key that enables Better Place to accept the up-front costs of ecosystem leadership and break the chicken-and-egg cycle we have seen stymie firms time and again.

In a world obsessed with globalization, size, and interconnectedness, it becomes ever more critical to know where to draw the boundaries. In this regard, Better Place is following the very same strategy of localized deployments that characterized the successful network technologies of yesteryear—the telegraph, the telephone, and the electric network itself were all initially deployed as local, isolated networks that were economically viable within their initial bounds, and were patched and linked together into broader networks only much later in their development. The first objective in an ecosystem is to put together the right pieces in the right place for enough customers to come on board and make the venture sustainable. The national and global network might come. But it will come later, after multiple successful deployments that gradually increase in scope, size, and ambition.

In this regard, Better Place's model does not preclude the rise of alternative approaches to commercializing EVs that might address problems A through F in a different way, relying on leasing arrangements and open systems. Success does not require or imply monopolization of a market. Just as we have multiple cell phone operators in the same geographies, nothing precludes multiple EV operators from sharing markets and even, through mechanisms analogous to cell phone roaming protocols, sharing infrastructure.

Reconfiguring Ecosystems for Success

The EV proposition is not a car problem, it is an ecosystem problem. And just like every success story we've encountered thus far, it needs an ecosystem solution. Sometimes this might be a matter of doing the same things better. But more often, it seems, success hinges on finding a way to do things differently by asking how we can modify a value blueprint: What can be separated? What can be combined? What can be relocated? What can be added? What can be subtracted?

Today, Better Place is taking its best shot at reconfiguring the electric car ecosystem. I find the company's example particularly instructive because it has used all five levers in combination to redraw the EV blueprint.

1. *Separate.* The central modification of the Better Place offer is the separation of the car from the battery, a move that

goes far in solving the stubborn problem of battery economics from the consumer's perspective.

2. *Combine.* By linking the battery, charging infrastructure, and the purchase of the electricity through the grid, Better Place gives the utilities the opportunity to serve more demand (and sell more power) without the need for new investment in capacity or distribution.

3. *Relocate.* In the traditional EV model, the burden of paying for electricity falls on the consumer. In the Better Place model, it is the company that manages the transaction with the power providers, allowing the consumer transaction to shift from kilowatt hours to miles driven.

4. *Add.* With its overarching operating system, Better Place adds a key component that facilitates energy management throughout the ecosystem. And because it has relieved the consumer from ownership of a specific battery, Better Place is able to introduce the battery switch station as a solution to the problem of driving range.

5. *Subtract.* With its operating system tying together the electric distribution system, the charging infrastructure, and the actual charging schedule of the batteries, Better Place is able to eliminate the need for a smart-grid infrastructure to solve the grid overload problem.

A Great Strategy Is a Good Start

Success, of course, is not guaranteed. Having a great value blueprint eliminates important sources of failure, but it does not, alas, ensure victory. Macroeconomic and geopolitical shocks pose existential risks to every enterprise. Moreover, although ecosystem problems A through F are solved "on paper," whether the solution will transfer to the harsh reality of the market will depend on Better Place's ability to manage a host of factors: getting the financial models right; managing its funding needs; setting the right price points; delivering the promised quality of service; overcoming the inevitable operational glitches and operational complexity, which is sure to accompany additional partners and service extensions; managing the organizational challenges that come with geographic expansions . . . the list goes on. But note that these factors are execution challenges. They are important concerns that will without doubt require excellent management and organization to successfully navigate. These are significant execution challenges. But, as such, their resolution falls largely, though not entirely, within Better Place's control.

A great blueprint structures the ecosystem in a way that minimizes co-innovation and adoption chain risk. The goal is not to eliminate risk—uncertainty is inherent in any innovation attempt. The goal is to shift risk into locations in which it can be managed most effectively.

At the very least, Better Place's efforts will be instructive. At the most, they will be truly transformative. I wish them great success.

CHAPTER 8

Sequencing Success:

Winning the Connected Game

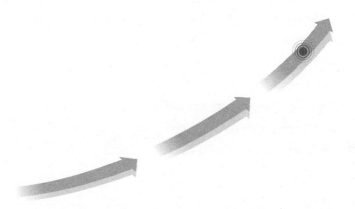

Winning in ecosystems requires winning more than just the execution race. It demands that you create coherent alignment among a network of partners, each of whom will succeed in their own execution, and each of whom is willing to collaborate productively with the other partners. How should you build this system?

More often than not, the answer is *gradually*. Constructing an ecosystem takes both time and direction. Like building any elegant structure, an ecosystem strategy requires a blueprint that lays out all the elements that will need to come together to create value. But it also requires a clear plan for the *sequence* in which the structure will be built.

In the world of product innovation, the standard development sequence transitions from the level of prototype (the development-stage notion of the value proposition) to pilot (a fully functional version of the final solution that is tested on a small, limited scale) to rollout (deploying the full value proposition at full scale). This approach is well suited to the world of stand-alone innovations, in which the construction of the offer itself is under your control.

But as we have seen time and again, the world of innovation ecosystems often requires a different approach. Here, the challenge is that delivering your value proposition requires multiple partners to agree, align, and commit. In this chapter we will consider an alternative pathway to scale. It is defined by three guiding principles for sequencing the successful construction of ecosystems:

1. *Minimum Viable Footprint (MVF)*—the smallest configuration of elements that can be brought together and still create unique commercial value.

2. *Staged Expansion*—the order in which additional elements can be added to the MVF so that each new element benefits from the system already in place and increases the value creation potential for the subsequent element to be added.

3. *Ecosystem Carryover*—the process of leveraging elements that were developed in the construction of one ecosystem to enable the construction of a second ecosystem.

I will illustrate these principles using examples of success in two industries. First, we will explore the way in which M-PESA, a

Kenya-based pioneer of mobile payments, followed these principles to build a financial services ecosystem that today is used by 65 percent of the Kenyan population. We will see how the combination of MVF and staged expansion offers a very different approach to commercialization and success than the usual mode of prototype-pilot-rollout.

We will then examine Apple's journey over the past decade as it redefined success, and reconfigured the ecosystem, in three distinct markets: music players, smartphones, and digital tablets. We will also see how Apple used MVF and staged expansion to create its position in each market, and we will uncover the hidden source of Apple's incredible success: the way it has applied the principle of ecosystem carryover to leverage elements and constellations from its old ecosystems to jump-start its construction of new ecosystems.

M-PESA: Creating Mobile Banking Services for Unbanked Populations

M-PESA is a joint venture between Vodafone and Safaricom, Kenya's dominant mobile network operator. Piloted in 2005, and then relaunched in 2007, it was built on a simple premise: use a (relatively) low-tech technology platform—SMS messaging—to enable money transfers by utilizing Safaricom's national network of agents. The proposition was inspired by the fact that, while 81 percent of Kenyans did not have access to a bank account, 27 percent of its citizens owned mobile phones, and an additional 27 percent had access to one—and those numbers were rapidly increasing. (By the end of 2010, 63 percent of Kenyans were mobile phone subscribers.) M-PESA sought to deliver a basic banking function to Kenya's huge unbanked population, facilitating commerce and entrepreneurship by increasing access to capital while reducing transaction costs—and to do it profitably.

In 2005, M-PESA (*M* is for "mobile" and *pesa* is Swahili for "cash") launched a pilot test of its proposition by partnering with a local microfinance institution, Faulu Kenya. Faulu Kenya, which distributed small loans to groups of small business borrowers who would then assume a collective responsibility to pay back the money, provided the customer base for the pilot program while M-PESA provided the technology and delivered the mobile services. The idea was to offer a comprehensive financial service that would let users transfer money person to person, deposit and withdraw cash through a Safaricom agent, and use M-PESA to receive and repay their micro-loans—all without the need for smartphones, 3G, or any other new technology development.

The service worked in much the same way as prepaid calling plans, where users can recharge their account by purchasing additional minutes from an agent and registering the transaction with the operator by sending an SMS message with a PIN code. In the case of mobile payments, the payee would receive an SMS text confirming that a payment had been registered on the network and a PIN code they could show to any Safaricom agent who would then disburse the cash. The idea was powerful, the market was big, and the need was real.

Despite an enthusiastic launch, the pilot program quickly ran into hurdles. "We had too many challenges to mention," said Vodafone's Susie Lonie, the project manager on the ground in Kenya. Although the execution challenge of developing the technology platform was manageable, the initiative depended on collaboration between the highly divergent cultures of telecom (forward-thinking, rapidly developing) and banking (conservative, slow to change), and lived in constant fear of being shut down by regulators. M-PESA's exact role—as a money transfer service, but also as

Figure 8.1: Value blueprint of M-PESA's 2005 pilot attempt.

an entity that allowed customers to maintain a noninterest-bearing account balance—was murky, given the fact that the company was not formally regulated as a financial institution.

More problematic were the hurdles that arose as a consequence of M-PESA's partnership with its microfinance partner. The involvement of Faulu Kenya meant that considerable complexity was added to the consumer transactions to accommodate its particular lending models, treasurer accounts, and accounting practices. Faulu Kenya, wary about the novelty of the M-PESA proposition, chose to retain its paper-based back-office procedures instead of adopting M-PESA's real-time data entry system. This resulted in a complex reconciliation process between the two organizations, which were moving at different speeds. According to Lonie: "The bottleneck in transferring the money M-PESA had collected in loan repayments to Faulu's bank account was getting its books to a point where it could request the funds. To make M-PESA more suitable for [microfinance institutions], we need to create data export files that can be easily uploaded in whatever format their existing software requires." The partnership between M-PESA and Faulu Kenya was a morass of interdependent processes that severely limited the success of the pilot study. Reflecting on the challenges of the experiment, Lonie recalled, "It was clear that we would need to find a way to simplify things before launching a national service for millions of customers."

Finding the Minimum Viable Footprint (MVF)

The M-PESA team went back to the drawing board and, in April 2007, launched a new initiative that took what had been a complex endeavor and focused only on its most basic elements. Instead of constructing the big picture all at once, M-PESA eliminated the key sources of coordination challenges—the banking component, which had introduced regulatory obstacles, and the micro-loan component, which had introduced the need to reconcile accounts across institutions—and instead constructed the simplest ecosystem it could assemble and still create some new value. It identified its *Minimum Viable Footprint* (MVF).

For M-PESA, the minimum viable footprint would be the money transfer service, which is the heart of the M-PESA promise. By sending a simple, secure text message to the network, M-PESA customers could transfer money to other mobile phone users anywhere in the country. Kenya was already blanketed with kiosks where Safaricom agents sold airtime to mobile customers, and these same agents

Minimum Viable Footprint

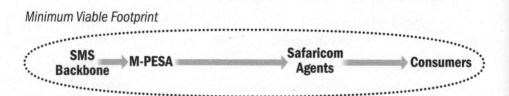

Figure 8.2: Value blueprint of M-PESA's 2007 relaunch—the minimum viable footprint (MVF) of the money transfer offer.

would facilitate the M-PESA money transfers, doling out the appropriate amount of cash to transfer recipients. And because no bank accounts were involved, the regulatory hurdles were much lower.

Of course, launching even just the money transfer service was not without its challenges. M-PESA still faced obstacles, high among which was ensuring that the rural agents maintained a sufficient cash float. Since customers tended to make deposits in the city to send to outlying regions, where their relatives would withdraw the funds, rural agents could easily run out of cash. The solution entailed a change in the way Safaricom agents worked together. But the relationship with Safaricom was strong; the technology was preestablished; the demand was palpable—the expected relative benefit overwhelmed the adjustment cost, and Safaricom embraced the change. By December 2007, approximately 1 million customers had signed up for the service.

A smart sequencing strategy does not miraculously eliminate all the challenges involved in building an ecosystem. But starting with the MVF allows you to begin with the subset of problems you are best positioned to solve—those with the lowest levels of risk and highest levels of partner motivation. And having solved these, you will be in a better position to manage the partnering challenges of the next stage of development.

From Minimum Viable Footprint to Staged Expansion

Having established a basic but demonstrably successful money transfer service, M-PESA began its staged expansion beyond its MVF, adding new partners to enhance the value of its core offer. It brought them on to its platform. And—unlike the pilot experience with Faulu Kenya, where the question of who will adjust to

Minimum Viable Footprint

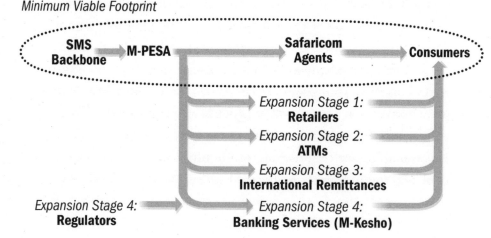

Figure 8.3: Value blueprint of M-PESA's 2007 relaunch showing the initial minimum viable footprint (MVF) and subsequent expansion stages of the offer.

whom was the subject of active and ultimately unproductive debate—it brought them there on its own terms.

Within the first year, M-PESA had partnered with a number of retailers and utilities, making it possible for customers to use their mobile phones to pay bills and buy goods (expansion stage 1). With its commercial legitimacy now clearly established, in 2008, the company forged a partnership with PesaPoint, one of the largest ATM service providers in Kenya. As an alternative to the Safaricom agents, M-PESA customers could now choose the option "ATM withdrawal" from the M-PESA menu on their phone and receive an ATM authorization code for one-time use; no bank card required (expansion stage 2). And in 2009, M-PESA, in partnership with Western Union, introduced an international remittance service to enable money transfers from the United Kingdom (expansion stage 3).

By July 2009, two years after its initial launch, M-PESA had expanded its customer base to 7.3 million, with an agent network of over 12,000. Cumulative person-to-person transfers had amounted to an impressive $2.7 billion (Kenya's GDP in 2009 was $63 billion). These strong numbers meant M-PESA was in a good position to expand its offering to add more formal banking services and insurance. This time, with proven commercial success and a history of reliable operation, the regulatory obstacle was much easier to cross.

In the spring of 2010, M-PESA did just that. In conjunction with Safaricom, the firm teamed up with Equity Bank, Kenya's biggest bank in terms of client base, to create M-Kesho (*kesho* is Swahili for "tomorrow"), a financial service that combines the benefits of a bank account with the convenience of M-PESA. M-PESA customers could now enjoy an interest-bearing bank account, as well as services such as micro-savings and micro-insurance, all of which could be accessed from their mobile phones (expansion stage 4). In voicing support for the venture, Equity Bank CEO Dr. James Mwangi stated, "We want to ensure that no Kenyan is locked out of accessing basic banking services. If you look at other solutions in the market, nobody has put together all these services to provide this kind of convenience to the customer."

By incorporating banking and microfinance services, M-PESA finally achieved the initial vision of the 2005 pilot program. Getting the value proposition right was not enough. Turning this vision into reality required a step-by-step approach: building initial value with an MVF offer (simple money transfer) and using it as a base for enhancing the core offer in a staged sequence (increasingly sophisticated money transfer).

A Choice of Paths: Pilots vs. Footprints

The M-PESA case offers a valuable contrast between two different approaches to building toward success. The path initially pursued by M-PESA in 2005, which was abandoned in the face of partner-induced complexity, exemplifies the traditional prototype-pilot-rollout approach to sequencing success: first, start with a prototype that offers a crude version of the full value proposition in order to test and validate the model; then, build a pilot trial that demonstrates the viability of the full value proposition on a small, testing scale; finally, launch the market rollout to deploy the full value proposition at full scale. The philosophy behind this approach is to validate the value proposition (prototype) and make sure it works in its entirety (pilot) before committing to scale (rollout). This makes a lot of sense in a world of products, where scaling is "simply" a matter of investing in volume production.

But in a world of ecosystems, the approach of scaling pilots is problematic—first, because it increases the extent of co-innovation and adoption chain risks that must be addressed from the get-go; and second, because even if the pilot demonstration is successful, aligning interdependent partners to simultaneously commit to a scaled rollout can be extremely challenging.* In the absence of a clear path to getting the system together at scale, ecosystem pilots languish and never get off the ground.

---

*   In the world of product development, a recent movement has been toward "lean start-up," a key technique of which is the minimum viable product (also referred to as the minimum feature set). The minimum viable product approach espouses market testing with bare-bones prototypes that allows for maximum learning from test customer feedback with the least amount of product development. This enables cheaper and faster iterations in the product development cycle. It contrasts with the philosophy of presenting (relatively) feature-rich prototypes that will allow test customers to offer more complete reactions.

The MVF is a different idea. It is not about learning or prototyping but rather about how to build collaboration and achieve scaled deployment. It is about looking at a value blueprint and identifying the leanest configuration of elements that can be brought together to create commercial value and serve as an ecosystem platform that can attract and accommodate, in stepwise fashion, the addition of later partners to build out the complete blueprint and fulfill the larger value proposition.

Underlying the failure of the initial M-PESA pilot effort was a combination of co-innovation and adoption chain challenges that were inherent in the nature of the value proposition (the need for regulatory approval, the need for accounting process reconciliation, etc.). But more than this, there was an inconsistent view of the venture's value blueprint and a disagreement about ecosystem leadership among all the partners. While there was consensus between the M-PESA and Faulu Kenya teams about the overall value proposition, there was no consensus on the specifics of how the different activities would actually come together and, just as important, whose organization and procedures would change to accommodate those of the other. This is typical in the early stages of ecosystem construction, and the greater the number of early partners, the higher the likelihood of competing visions and aspirations.

Staged expansion from an MVF presents a very different path. Rather than the piloting approach of scaling up a fully developed value proposition, the MVF approach means that the innovator first rolls out a basic value proposition at commercial scale and only then moves to enhance the value proposition to its full potential in a series of staged expansions. The difference—in terms of leadership clarity, blueprint cohesion, and partner management— is staggering.

The MVF is focused on achieving commercial scale early—a broad deployment of a (relatively) shallow offer. With this as an established foundation, the conversation with potential partners shifts from "after we jointly get this system together, we'll go find customers and then we'll all succeed" to "I have an established customer pool that would appreciate the value proposition even more if you were a part of it." By establishing a base of consumers, the MVF reduces (but does not eliminate) demand uncertainty for partners and lowers the hurdles to bringing them on board. In

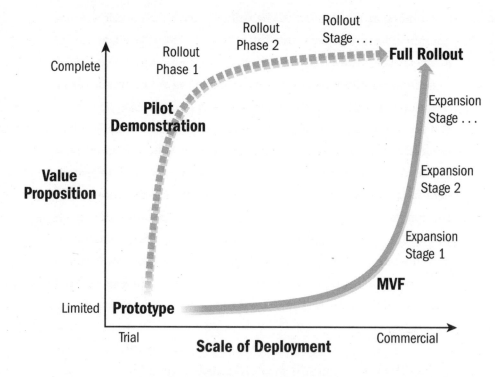

Figure 8.4: Alternative paths to reaching full-scale ecosystem deployment contrasting a traditional pilot demonstration followed by a phased rollout and a minimum viable footprint (MVF) rollout followed by a staged expansion.

the language of the leadership prism we discussed in chapter 5, building out in stages from the MVF kernel makes it easier to convince partners of their expected surplus. And the organization that drives the MVF establishes itself as the de facto ecosystem leader—both because it has clear ownership of the customer base and because it is in control of the order in which additional partners will be invited to come on board.

M-PESA's 2007 money-transfer-only offer had all the characteristics of a perfect minimum viable footprint. It was *simple,* and therefore relatively straightforward to deploy; it was *valued,* and therefore able to attract demand among an initial group of target consumers; and it was *extendable,* and therefore able to accommodate the addition of new elements. Having established itself in the market, M-PESA was able to use this MVF as a platform on which to sequentially mount additional elements for the expansion of the proposition.

The hallmark of smart sequencing is that overcoming the challenges in each intermediate stage achieves two functions. First, it creates immediate value: each stage delivers a sustainable commercial proposition on its own. Second, it reduces subsequent challenges: achievements along the sequence are cumulative, such that progress in one stage feeds directly into progress in the next. By sequencing the construction of an ambitious ecosystem into a series of discrete stages, M-PESA was able to plot an incremental path to radical change.

Ecosystem Carryover: How to Build Success upon Success

Driving staged expansion from an MVF is a powerful pathway to success. And continued expansion within the ecosystem is a compelling avenue to continued growth. Building a successful ecosystem, however, offers an additional strategy lever: *Ecosystem Carryover,* leveraging your success in constructing one ecosystem to create advantage in constructing a new ecosystem.

We can see the principle of ecosystem carryover underlying many successful transformations. For example, in the mid-1980s, Hasbro seized on the marketing formula of supporting its action figure toy lines (like G.I. Joe and Transformers) with comic-book stories and televised cartoon series. Twenty years later, it recognized the potential to carry over these elements from the toy ecosystem to create a new position in the media ecosystem. Taking its toys-turned-characters, their powerful brands, and the extensive mythology developed for the television series, it approached the Hollywood studios with the idea of playing an active role in developing feature movies around these characters. While the toy-movie link had been well established since the days of Disney and *Star Wars,* Hasbro's initiative marked a major reversal of the relationship between the studios and the toy manufacturers. In the past, studios would create the movies and then license the various merchandizing rights to toy companies. This was the first time that a toy maker would take the leadership role, using its carryover to drive the moviemaking process, and capturing a much bigger share of the gains in return.

Medtronic, a leading medical device manufacturer and pioneer in cardiac rhythm management, has similarly pursued a combination of carryover and reconfiguration to create opportunities in new therapeutic markets. In a series of staged expansions from its MVF in pacemakers, it broadened its footprint within the cardiology sector to add integrated monitoring and diagnostic services. In doing so, it shifted its position from product supplier to health-care delivery partner. It expanded its links beyond cardiologists and patients to create new interactions with additional members of the hospital ecosystem, including information technology professionals, hospital administrators, and insurers. In parallel, it found ways to carry over elements from this expanded cardiology ecosystem to make inroads into new areas of the medical sector like neurology and endocrinology with innovative technology solutions like neurostimulation and implantable drug delivery systems.

FedEx's growth from overnight shipping to orchestrating a range of supply chain and inventory management services, eBay's extension from online auction house (its original MVF) to virtual shopping mall to e-payment broker (PayPal) to creditor (Bill Me

Later), Facebook's expansion from social network to media platform, and Amazon's creation of business-to-business service offers alongside its retail operations were all driven by the same fundamental principles of MVF, staged expansion, and ecosystem carryover. Beyond a clear focus on their own capabilities, these firms were meticulous in their approach to configuring external elements *around* those capabilities. But while we can see these three principles employed by scores of successful organizations, no recent firm is a better exemplar of their use than Apple.

Apple's Success in the New Millennium

Everyone knows that Apple has been on an incredible run for the last decade. But while a great deal of attention has focused on Apple's sleek product designs, what is often misunderstood is Apple's systematic approach to its ecosystem strategy—its hidden source of advantage.

Apple has no monopoly on great products, great interfaces, or a great brand. Apple's product design is key, of course, but Apple's rivals have been at its heels—behind but close—for years, even garnering praise for comparable design quality and better functionality. In awarding the Consumer Electronics Show 2006 prize for Best in Show, CNET's editors commented, "iPod killer? With a brighter screen, better battery life, and more features, the Creative Zen Vision:M certainly has the goods to give the iPod a run for its money." In 2009, *Wall Street Journal* tech guru Walt Mossberg said of the Palm Pre: "It's a beautiful, innovative and versatile hand-held computer that's fully in the iPhone's class." The following year, *New York Times* "State of the Art" columnist David Pogue remarked on the "gorgeous" Samsung Galaxy Tablet: "The dawn of the would-be iPad is upon us. . . . the Android tablet concept represents more than just a lame effort to grab a slice of tablet hype. As with Android phones, it represents an alternative that's different enough to justify its existence." Apple diehards will argue that Apple design is twice as good as the competition—but even that does not explain why the company's market share is an order of magnitude greater than that of any other rival.

Nor is Apple unique in attempting to lead an ecosystem around its offers. A slew of high-tech blue chips—Nokia, Palm, Samsung, Sony, Cisco, Hewlett-Packard, Research in Motion, Google, Microsoft— pursued these same objectives for their various offers, with great vigor and, often, far greater resources. But as of the time of this writing not one has yet come close to Apple's success.

The reason for this lies in the fact that, although all these firms share the very same objectives, Apple has pursued them in a highly distinctive way. No less distinctive than its products, but far less understood, has been Apple's approach to innovating its ecosystems. And while Apple's ability to create its MVF and then stage its expansion has been exceptional, my own view is that it is Apple's mastery of the principle of ecosystem carryover that has propelled it so far ahead of its rivals. Its hidden point of differentiation has not been in its elegant products but rather in its approach to leveraging its advantage from one ecosystem into the next—a feat it has repeated as it extended its reach from MP3 players to smartphones to, most recently, tablet devices. How long its unique success will last is unclear. But its approach is timeless.

iPod: Staged Expansion

While the 1990s were rocky for former Apple CEO Steve Jobs, in the new century it seemed he could do no wrong. In chapter 6 we saw how Jobs constructed the iPod ecosystem. For his minimum viable footprint he carried over two elements from the Macintosh world—the Apple Store and the iTunes music management software—and waited for the other key elements—broadband and content—to arrive before he introduced his MP3 player into the marketplace. In 2001, the iPod player was rolled out. The MVF was in place.

Apple's first expansion of the iPod ecosystem came with the rollout of the iTunes music store in 2003, which offered consumers an easy way to purchase legal digital music. The next expansion was to open the iPod platform to non-Mac users (almost inexplicably, the iPod was designed as a Mac-only product, and it took two years before Apple launched an iPod that could be enjoyed by the 90 percent of the world that used Windows and USB ports). This was followed by a series of exciting new iPod generations like the iPod Mini, Shuffle, Nano, and added features like video playback. Although the initial launch of the iPod was

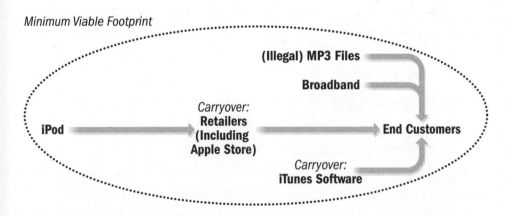

Figure 8.5: Value blueprint of Apple's iPod—the minimum viable footprint (MVF) of the music player offer.

greeted with skepticism, within four years it was heralded as a monumental triumph.

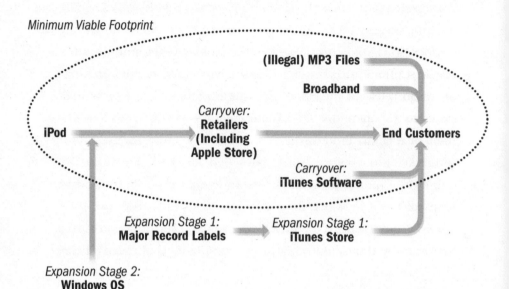

Figure 8.6: Value blueprint of Apple's iPod offer showing the sequence in which the ecosystem was constructed—minimum viable footprint (MVF) followed by online music store (expansion stage 1) followed by compatibility with the Windows operating system (expansion stage 2).

Enter the iPhone

By 2007, the unforeseen triumph of Apple's iPod, boasting 100 million customers, had transformed Apple into a tech darling. Consumers and the media alike eagerly awaited the company's next offering, and from January to June of that year, Apple's stock shot up 44 percent in anticipation of a smartphone that would repeat the iPod's success. At 6 p.m. on June 29, the iPhone, Apple's entrant into the crowded smartphone field, was launched to a media frenzy. Jobs clearly saw the potential for profit: "It's a huge market. I mean, a billion phones get shipped every year, and that's almost an order of magnitude greater than the number of music players. It's four times the number of PCs that ship every year."

Still, success was not obvious. Smartphones were not a new proposition. Nokia had launched the Nokia 9000 Communicator, the first phone with Internet connectivity, back in 1996. In 2000, Ericsson released the R380, the initial mobile device to be marketed as a smartphone. A year later, Palm followed up with its version of a smartphone—the first to gain widespread use in the United States. And in 2002, a wave of devices hit the market: Research in Motion's BlackBerry, Sony Ericsson's P800 (the first smartphone to feature a camera), and Handspring's Palm OS Treo (a combination cell phone–organizer–Internet terminal that also ran the thousands of Palm-compatible applications available for download online).

Once again, Jobs was late—five years late. And rivals didn't seem to care. Reacting to Apple's January 2007 announcement of the iPhone (six months before its launch), Jim Balsillie, co-CEO of BlackBerry shrugged, "It's kind of one more entrant into an already very busy space with lots of choice for consumers. But in terms of a sort of a sea-change for BlackBerry, I would think that's overstating it."

Yes, it was beautifully designed, with a host of new features—a multi-touch screen interface, an innovative accelerometer, a full Web browser, novel applications like Google Maps and YouTube. But while it was highly advanced in some features, the iPhone was well behind the curve in others—a substandard still-image camera, an inability to record video, and shockingly, though launched as a data device six years after the start of the 3G revolution, the iPhone was a 2G dinosaur (the 3G version didn't arrive until July 2008). Even more shocking, the phone was exclusively available from only one carrier in each country where it was launched (AT&T in the United States, T-Mobile in Germany, Orange in France, O2 in the United Kingdom, and Softbank in Japan). In a representative assessment, *New York Times* technology columnist David Pogue noted, "The bigger problem is the AT&T network. In a *Consumer Reports* study, AT&T's signal ranked either last or second to last in 19 out of 20 major cities. . . . You have to use AT&T's ancient EDGE cellular network, which is excruciatingly slow." For years, users and reviewers alike would skewer AT&T for an epidemic of dropped voice calls at peak usage hours.

And retailing at $499 (with a two-year contract), the phone was significantly more expensive than any of the competition: Samsung's UpStage phone, a smartphone that also included a music player, was priced at a mere $99 in 2007; HTC's Touch, which included a touch screen, Wi-Fi connectivity, and Internet browsing, was priced at $250 with a two-year contract from Sprint. Finally, the iPhone took the idea of a closed platform to the extreme. In a press release, the company announced that any attempt to install a non-Apple application on the phone would void the warranty. Moreover, Apple warned that attempts to unlock the phone from the AT&T network would "cause irreparable damage to the iPhone's software, which will likely result in the modified iPhone becoming permanently inoperable when a future Apple-supplied iPhone software update is installed." Apple threatened to turn your $499 iPhone into a $499 iBrick! And it did!

Asked to react to the announcement of the iPhone, Microsoft CEO Steve Ballmer literally laughed out loud, "Five hundred dollars fully subsidized with a plan! I said that's the most expensive phone in the world, and it doesn't appeal to business customers because it doesn't have a keyboard, which makes it not a very good e-mail machine. . . . We have great Windows Mobile devices on the market today. . . . I look at that [the iPhone] and I say I like our strategy. I like it a lot."

But even as the competition laughed, Steve Jobs smiled. Within its first year of sales—and thirteen months before the advent of the App Store—6 million iPhones were sold. (And Apple could have sold more: the phone's popularity meant they ran out of the older model six weeks before the July 2008 launch of the iPhone 3G.) What did Jobs see that his rivals didn't?

Ecosystem Carryover: The Hidden Key to Apple's Success

When Jobs launched the iPhone, he didn't just launch a beautifully designed phone that had a built-in iPod. Nor was it just a phone with an iPod and iTunes management software. Nor was it just a phone with an iPod, iTunes management, and wireless access to the iTunes Store. He carried over this entire constellation of iPod elements and one thing more: every iPod user's entire library of music, playlists, album covers . . . it was not just the iPod elements that carried over, it was your entire iPod history.

Steve Jobs could smile because he knew what this ecosystem carryover meant. Of the 22 million iPods sold during the 2007 holiday season, 60 percent went to buyers who already owned at least one iPod. The iPhone was not going to be a new entrant fighting to capture attention in a crowded mobile phone market. It was the next-generation iPod. By carrying over the key elements of the iPod ecosystem, he would carry over his buyers too.

Notice that the principle of ecosystem carryover does *not* hinge on notions of switching costs or customer lock-in. The underlying philosophy behind those tactics is one of preventing end consumers from moving to rival offers. Their focus is on securing an existing position. In contrast, the intent of ecosystem carryover is to induce existing consumers and partners to participate in new value propositions.

Using Ecosystem Carryover to Drive Ecosystem Reconfiguration

On its own, this iPhone-as-next-iPod strategy enabled by ecosystem carryover would ensure that the iPhone would be a success with Apple's consumers. But knowing you have a hit on your hands is one thing; knowing what to do with it is quite another.

The mobile phone industry had already seen blockbusters—Motorola's RAZR, introduced in late 2003, sold over 50 million units just within its first two years; Nokia's model 1100 sold over 200 million units between 2003 and 2007. These hits grew the mobile pie.

In contrast, Jobs would use his hit to change the mobile game. He would use his carryover from the music ecosystem to reconfigure the smartphone ecosystem, and in so doing, he would ensure that the iPhone would be a blockbuster for Apple shareholders.

The smartphone ecosystem was well developed by the time the iPhone launched, and the links among the actors were well established: mobile phone producers (Nokia, Motorola) sell their phones to various operators (AT&T, Sprint, Vodafone) who then package the phone with a calling plan and compete to sell it to consumers.

With the iPhone, however, Apple would reconfigure the ecosystem, adding new elements and redrawing links across the blueprint. It began with exclusivity. Apple would partner with only one operator in any country. (In the United States, Apple initially awarded a five-year exclusivity deal to AT&T, an agreement that was subsequently amended to allow rival operators to offer the iPhone in

2011.) This was a huge boon to the favored candidate: operators had long struggled to differentiate their offers, but with everyone offering the same handsets, customer loyalty and pricing power were both elusive as cell phone users hopped from one contract to the next, seeking lower rates, newer phones, and higher subsidies. And here was Apple, offering not just exclusive access to the most talked-about phone in history, but also exclusive access to Apple consumers—the most desirable customer segment imaginable (during the course of a two-year contract, the average iPhone user paid AT&T $2,000—$83 per month—double the amount paid by the average mobile phone user). And Apple would actively enforce this exclusivity on behalf of the operator by rendering modified phones inoperable through software updates—the iBrick threat. Not only would Apple deliver the customers to you as the operator, but they would guarantee to keep them away from your rivals.

Apple would also redefine the nature of the relationship between the handset maker and the operator. Unlike the usual supplier-buyer relationship between handset makers and operators, this was to be a partnership—with Apple as senior partner. While there would be a transfer of product from Apple to the mobile operator, there would also be a clear link between Apple and the consumers: they may be using your network, but they are our customers. Signing on as the exclusive operator meant signing away a lot of control—over marketing decisions and budgets, over the phone interface, and over the customer. And it also meant signing away revenue—after paying Apple for the phone, the operator would need to share a portion of every iPhone user's monthly bill, estimated to be as high as $18 per user per month.* But the reward

---

* In the United States, AT&T announced the end of the revenue share—in exchange for higher up-front payments to Apple—in June of 2008, coinciding with the launch of the iPhone 3G.

was high as well—around the world, high-end customers flocked to the iPhone operators. A successful ecosystem leader makes sure that followers win too.

The two-part secret to the iPhone's early success was not that it was a great phone (it was, but this was not a secret) and not that it had an app store (that came later). First, the iPhone strategy explicitly carried over the iPod ecosystem and with it the iPod users. The iPhone started life with a built-in customer base. True, other firms had introduced new phones for which everyone in the industry had great expectations. But none of these predecessors had made the conceptual leap from strategizing better products to strategizing better ecosystems. Second, Steve Jobs—a master of the game—did more than just carry over his loyal customer base from one market to then next. Like Hasbro with the movie studios, he leveraged this crucial carryover to reconfigure the ecosystem, shifting his position from supplier to partner, to secure unprecedented control and an unprecedented deal with the mobile operators.

Staged Expansion of the iPhone Ecosystem

A year after the iPhone's launch, Apple extended its ecosystem with the introduction of the App Store, an official platform through which users could finally download applications without fear of incapacitating their phone, and through which eager developers could finally present their programs to the world, and (potentially) profit from them. Apple released a software development kit for the iPhone in March 2008, and in July of that year the App Store was officially launched, offering 500 apps. Six months later, 5 million apps had been downloaded, and on January 22, 2011, Apple announced its 10 billionth app download. The App Store was another masterstroke. It made the device an evergreen

Minimum Viable Footprint

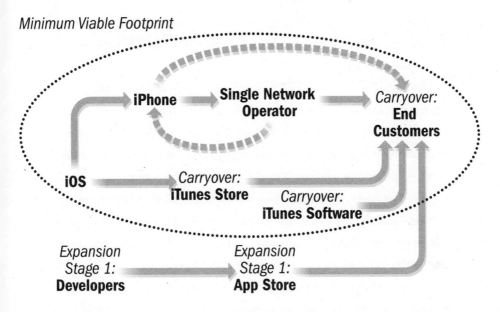

Figure 8.7: Value blueprint of Apple's iPhone offer showing the carryover elements from the iPod ecosystem and new links that comprised the minimum viable footprint followed by the addition of the App Store.

proposition that could, with the tap of a finger, become ever more useful, more entertaining, and more customized to each individual user. It shifted the basis of smartphone customization from the manufacturer's design of the hardware to the user's own choices in selecting software.

Staging expansion in this way allowed Apple to leverage partner collaboration while still preserving—for better or worse—almost complete control. The company retained strict jurisdiction over which apps it sold and which apps would be excluded from the platform. And the reason Apple was able to dictate terms to yet another community is directly linked to the success it created with the MVF *before* allowing the app developers to participate in the ecosystem. This approach of sequencing is at the heart of its approach to ecosystem leadership.

The iPad: Pioneering with Ecosystem Carryover

With the launch of the iPad in April 2010, Apple once again leveraged its success in one domain—phones—to drive success in another—tablets. But unlike the iPod and the iPhone, both of which were late arrivals in existing product categories, the iPad was an attempt to pioneer a new market space, "a third category of device, between a smartphone and a laptop," as Jobs explained during a product event in January 2010. The iPad is a tablet "device" (not quite a computer, but far more than an e-reader), marketed to offer an enhanced multimedia experience. Users can watch videos, read books and magazines, access apps, listen to music, organize photos, play games, and browse the Web, all on a sleek device.

Despite the physical similarity to the iPhone from a product perspective, from an ecosystem perspective, the iPad was a major strategy departure for Apple. With both the iPod and the iPhone, Apple launched products with value that was high on a standalone basis. Apple could establish the MVF with a minimal set of partners (none in the case of the iPod; just the mobile operator in the case of the iPhone). External partners clamored to join the party once it got going, but their support was neither needed nor welcomed at the start.

In stark contrast, the iPad is, at heart, a conduit for non-Apple content. For it to offer sufficient content to attract consumers, Apple had to convince publishers to take a bet on the device. Although Jobs was able to carry over the elements from the earlier ecosystems (the iTunes Store and the App Store), for the iPad to be anything more than an oversize iPod Touch, content from books, magazines, and newspapers had to be there from the beginning. The iPad was the first time that Apple confronted the need to start its journey with a host of initial partners. And to enable this process, Jobs carried over the newest asset that was created by the runaway success of the iPhone: the intense media hype that surrounded his every move. Eight months in advance of the iPad's formal announcement in January 2010—and eleven months before its actual April launch—financial analysts, technology blogs, and the mainstream media were already obsessed. "It could be Apple's latest billion-dollar jackpot," the *Observer* speculated. According to the *New York Times*, "2010 Could be the Year of the Tablet." And in the months between the formal announcement and the launch, Jobs fed the frenzy like a true media master: "There are already 75 million people who know how to use this because of how many iPhones and iPod Touches we've shipped." Once again, there were millions of customers in his pocket, he implied, just waiting to get their hands on the next exciting device. Who's coming aboard?

Publishers couldn't resist Jobs's siren call, and they dug deep in their pockets to create iPad-specific content. By the 2010 launch, Penguin, HarperCollins, Simon & Schuster, Macmillan, and the Hachette Group had all committed to providing books for the device, risking their relationship with Amazon. The *New York Times* agreed to publish a daily version of the paper specially tailored for iPad users. Rupert Murdoch even created an iPad-only newspaper, the *Daily*, "from scratch," as he put it. And Condé Nast created iPad-only digital versions of its *New Yorker, Glamour, GQ,* and *Vanity Fair* magazines. Charles H. Townsend, president and chief executive of Condé Nast, said, "We feel confident enough that consumers will want our content in this new format that we are committing the resources necessary to be there."

With a clear view of its MVF, Apple attracted the partners it needed in order to make the iPad a compelling proposition for consumers. It is interesting to note that, in signing up for the iPad,

Minimum Viable Footprint

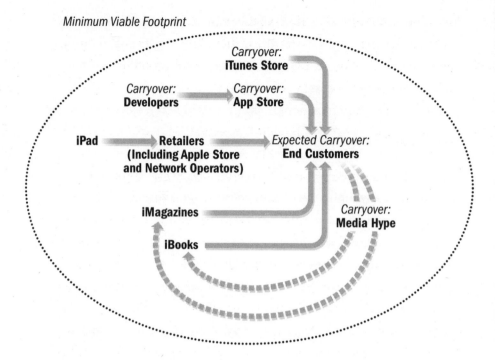

Figure 8.8: Value blueprint of Apple's iPad minimum viable footprint.

media partners were taking on a somewhat asymmetric risk. Publishers—always eager for a new sales outlet—were counting on the iPad to deliver millions of readers willing to pay for digital content. On the surface, this sounds like a fair deal. But think back to our followership discussion in chapter 5. The smart follower asks himself whether a potential leader makes money the same way he does. If the answer is no, then interests may be misaligned. With the iPad, Apple makes its money the moment a customer buys the device, which the promise of content has already convinced many millions to do. For the cash-strapped publishers, however, the up-front investment in reengineering their product, adding in-depth videos, interactive graphics, audio interviews, and myriad other features is only recouped on an issue-by-issue basis. For them, the question is not just whether consumers will flock to the iPad; it is whether, having paid for the iPad, these consumers will then be eager to spend—and spend consistently—on the content they have custom developed for the tablet.

Ecosystem Leadership: Noblesse Oblige

This last point, however, points to a challenge for Apple and, for that matter, any highly successful ecosystem leader.

As critical to Apple's continued success as managing competition with its rivals will be its ability to sustain productive relationships with its partners. Apple's 2011 demand of a 30 percent commission on all subscriptions transacted on its platform was regarded by many partners as egregiously high, leading to public fallouts with content providers like the Financial Times, and cries of "Economically untenable," in the words of one partner who then noted, "There are other platforms out there." This is a major risk, one faced by any highly successful ecosystem leader—Apple and developers; Amazon and publishers; Hollywood studios and cinemas. As power grows, and grows asymmetrically, so too does the potential for abuse, intended or accidental. A leader who loses its followers loses its leadership. As success grows, so does the need not only to create but also to share enough surplus to keep partners engaged, productive, and, to the extent possible, loyal.

The Stepwise Path to Success: Beyond Diversification

Building a robust ecosystem is a progression that marries smart timing and smart strategy. Start by identifying your minimum viable footprint: what is the smallest configuration of core elements needed for your offering to create unique value? Assess the most advantageous order in which to add elements to expand the ecosystem: what element offers the best balance of enhancing the preexisting system and acting as a building block for subsequent expansion? Finally, consider what constellation within the current ecosystem can be carried over to help establish an MVF for a new value proposition and a new ecosystem.

In a product-focused world, much advice for diversification has concentrated on optimally exploiting core competencies. An early poster child was Canon, which was able to leverage its capabilities in optics and micro-mechanics and enter a broad range of markets, from cameras, printers, fax machines, and copiers, all the way to semiconductor lithography equipment. But a narrow focus on competence misses a critical dimension of the growth strategies of many of today's leading firms.

Replicating Apple's core capabilities in product design and component integration would not replicate their position in either current or future markets—it was not the innovative touch screen or elegant interface that drove successive wins in music players, phones, and tablets. They were necessary, but they were not sufficient.

This wide-lens view of Apple's success has seemed lost on many of Apple's rivals. In the rush to match the pieces, they have missed the critical connections that draw the entire ecosystem together into a coherent whole. They have brought plenty of money, talent, and ambition to the competition, but with few exceptions (most notably Amazon), as of the time of this writing their strategies have brought little in the way of ecosystem carryover to jump-start their value propositions. For this reason, they seem to start from scratch in new endeavors in smartphones, music players, and tablets, paying a high ante for their entry and a high subsidy for partner support.

Focused on matching the discrete elements of the value

proposition, competitors press to grow the number of apps in their app stores, to create their own music download services, to incorporate their own multi-touch interfaces. Not enough, and not the point. It was Apple's differentiated strategy for constructing its ecosystem that allowed the company to move so effectively from offering great products to delivering great solutions. And it was the consistent drive to leverage elements from one value proposition to the next, always with an eye on the MVF, staged expansion, carryover, and reconfiguration, that has allowed Apple to extend its advantage from one realm to the next.

The principles of the MVF, staged expansion, and ecosystem carryover are at the core of successful ecosystem strategy, regardless of industry or sector. They shed a clarifying light on success in an interdependent world and, I hope, on your own strategy as well.

CHAPTER 9

Multiplying Your Odds
of Success

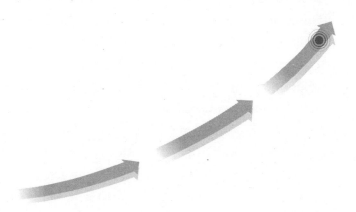

In the new world of innovation ecosystems, our ability to execute on our initiatives no longer determines our success. Traditional concerns about our competencies, consumers, and rivals are still critical, but now our strategies and actions must also account for interdependence. Those who master its principles will capture outsize gains. Those who ignore its implications will be penalized with greater inefficiencies, lags, and disappointments.

The Wide-Lens Toolbox

The tools introduced in this book will give you a wide lens through which to assess your strategies and with which to guide your actions and commitments. Using them actively will help ensure that you see the entire ecosystem on which your success depends. And, having exposed your issues before they become problems, the tools will allow you to make better decisions and more effective investments.

STEP 1

Begin by gaining a clear view of your *Value Blueprint*. This is a crucial first step in winning the ecosystem game. Drawing your blueprint will help you and your team articulate a shared vision not only of your value proposition but also of the way to bring it about. It will reveal hidden *Co-innovation Risks* and *Adoption Chain Risks*. It will surface missing pieces and mismatched assumptions, and help you strategize your role, your timing, and your approach to creating advantage.

Mapping your ecosystem will force you to be explicit about the links and dependencies that you are building into your plans. There is nothing inherently wrong with dependence, as long you know it is there from the start. Drawing a clear blueprint will encourage you and your team to formulate a plan for dealing with problematic elements proactively, at the start of your journey. It will help you avoid the familiar improvisation of tactical adjustments that is the hallmark of incomplete strategy.

STEP 2

With your blueprint clearly articulated, you are in a position to ask key questions about which role you want to play and when you want to make your move. Using the *Leadership Prism* to assess the distribution of expected surplus will help you identify who the natural ecosystem leadership candidates are, and whether you are among them. Using the *First-mover Matrix* will help you determine your ideal timing, letting you see whether the structure of interdependence is likely to reward early movers or hold them at the starting line waiting for the race to start.

STEP 3

The way in which you bring the necessary elements together can be a source of enormous advantage in a world of interdependence. Exploring alternative blueprints using the *Five Levers of Ecosystem Reconfiguration* will help you arrive at a plan that can accept the constraints of your ecosystem and still deliver a complete value proposition. And coupling this exercise with the principles of the *Minimum Viable Footprint, Staged Expansion,* and *Ecosystem Carryover* will help you identify the best sequence to follow in building toward your value proposition, and then leverage this achievement to extend your advantage to additional opportunities.

These tools are meant to be used iteratively, to help you and your team converge on the best strategy you can create. Use them when you start a new initiative, but also at different stages of its deployment, as a way of making sure that the full ecosystem is on track and to continuously seek more advantageous pathways to success.

The wide-lens tool kit will expose your blind spots and let you see problems before they arise. Part of what this means, however, is that you will see more problems. The unproductive reaction is to feel disempowered because recognizing all the new sources of failure can sap the will for action. The productive reaction, in contrast, is to embrace this wider view, accept the world for what it is—a challenging place in which to succeed—and find your best path to success. The purpose of this book is not for you to close these pages and say, "Innovation is a high-risk game, and therefore I shouldn't play." Instead, my hope is that you conclude, "Innovation is a high-risk game, but now that I see where the risks lie, and know how to mitigate them, I feel more confident in choosing the surest path toward success."

Knowing the Risks and Multiplying the Odds

At the heart of this book is a simple suggestion: before diving too deeply into a new initiative, make sure you understand the ecosystem into which you will need to integrate for your efforts to even have a chance at success. If you begin the innovation process by looking at the innovation ecosystem, and your place in it, it is possible to avoid investing time and resources in endeavors that were doomed from the beginning. Developing a better understanding of the odds is the key to making better bets.

Consider an industry where innovation success rates are low—assume 10 percent. (If you're in services, your natural odds are much higher; if you're in pharmaceuticals, they are much lower—but regardless of your industry, the logic will be the same.) With firms putting out their best efforts, doing their traditional due diligence, and focusing on execution, ten out of a hundred innovation efforts meet their expectations and succeed. Ninety out of the hundred fail. These are the unadulterated odds. This is why we talk about innovation as a high-risk activity. The good news, of course, is that if 10 percent is the industry norm, then that's all we need to stay in the game.

What we want, however, is to thrive in the game. And this requires doing better than the benchmark. The standard approach to improving innovation is to exhort managers to execute better, teams to be more effective, marketers to be more creative (all, of course, while staying within budget). Let's assume it works: through sheer force of will, the organization is able to deliver twice as many successful innovations as before.

Notice two characteristics of this approach. First, if it works, our odds double to 20 percent—we still lose on eighty out of the hundred innovation initiatives. Second, it requires a miracle.

The wide-lens tools offer an alternative approach, one that will first help us make better choices and then better manage the initiatives we choose to pursue. In looking at the hundred initiatives the organization has decided to pursue, it is clear that all are promising ideas, appealing to consumers and pursued by motivated teams (if this were not the case, we would not be investing in them). But it is impossible to tell which ten will succeed. When we use a wide lens to examine these initiatives and take their ecosystems into consideration, an amazing thing happens. We still cannot tell which ten will succeed—we cannot escape the role of luck as the arbiter of winners. But we can make some pretty strong predictions about which fifty will lose. Not because they are bad ideas, or are being managed by bad teams, but because, from the start, the structure of their ecosystems is set to undermine their success. Their value blueprints are clogged with red and yellow lights that will keep them from having a chance to win regardless of how well you execute your part.

Wherever we see these flagrant ecosystem obstacles, we can avoid the bet. We are still left with the ten winners but need not waste our scarce resources on the fifty initiatives that were doomed from the start: we avoid the predictable failures and make only the top fifty bets. Ten out of fifty brings us to 20 percent *without* the need for a miracle.

Making only half the bets means freeing up resources that we can now allocate to the top fifty. Within the original resource budget, we can double management focus. We can double the marketing spend. With twice the resources on every initiative, combined with more time and attention to crafting a robust value blueprint and nurturing the ecosystem, we don't need a miracle to double the wins. At twenty out of fifty we are at 40 percent in a realistic way—and four times more effective than the benchmark.

This is the path: eliminate avoidable failure; strategize more robust success.

A Closing Wish

Eliminating the blind spots of interdependence is everybody's problem. Whether you are a CEO, an investor, or project team member; in a large multinational or an emergent start-up; in the corporate sector or at a nonprofit: if you are contributing to a collaborative effort, then your success depends not just on your own efforts but also on your partners' ability, willingness, and likelihood to succeed.

Each of us is an investor, responsible for allocating our own time and effort across multiple opportunities and competing demands. Many of us are further responsible for allocating other people's resources as well—their labor, their capital, and their attention. With every new undertaking, every new initiative, we are taking risks with these resources. Our goal is to make the best possible choices across a portfolio of opportunities that leave us— and those who depend on us—better off.

My hope is that this book offers you a broad perspective to help you navigate the new and changing world of interdependence. By applying the wide-lens principles, you will be better able to expose the hidden sources of dependence that lurk beneath the surface of a strategy and be better equipped to manage them proactively and productively. You will construct better plans, and then deploy them with teams that share a more coherent vision of where they are trying to go and how they are going to get there.

Luck will always play a role in driving outcomes. In this spirit, I wish you, first, good luck. And second, that the wise application of the wide-lens principles means you will need less of it.

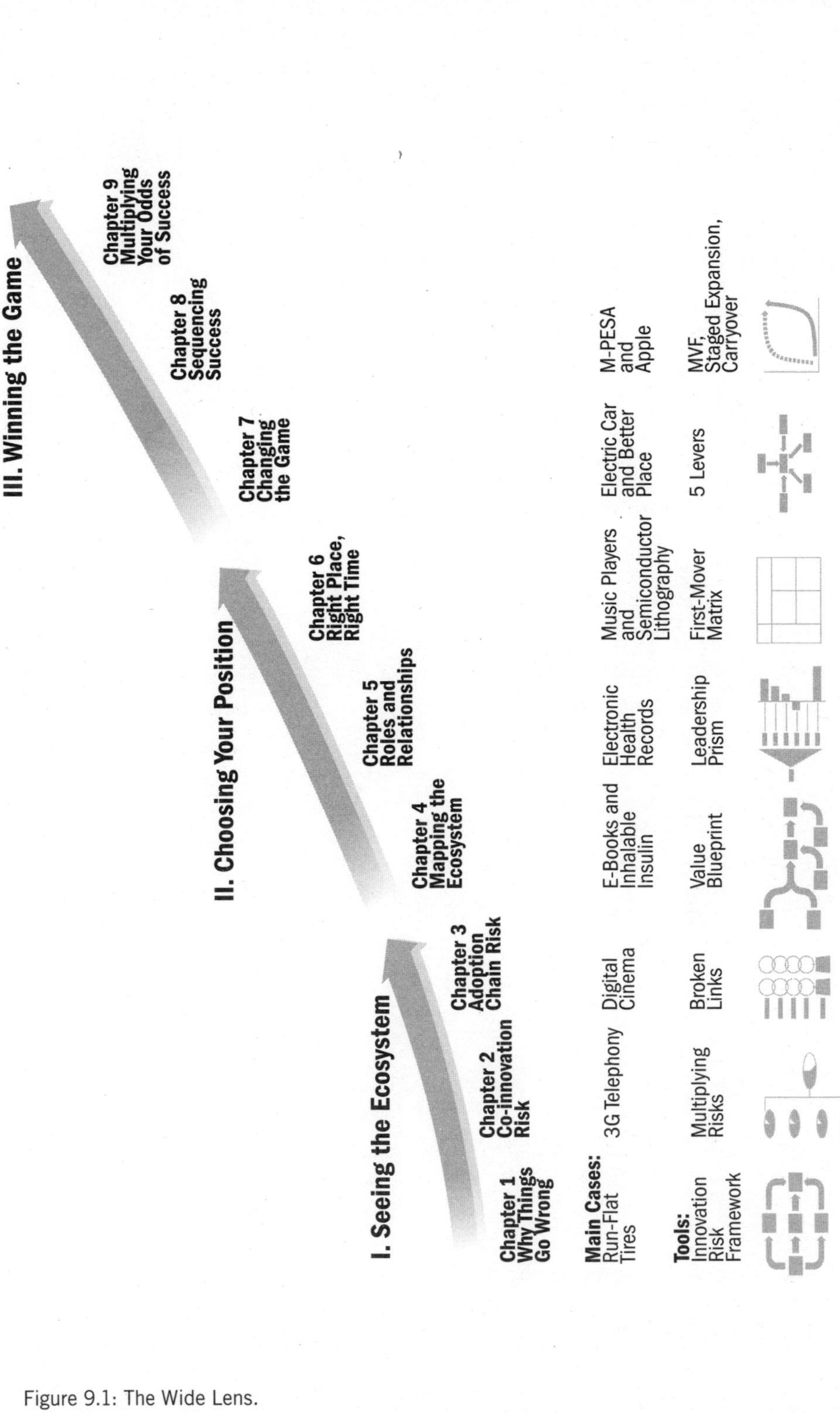

Figure 9.1: The Wide Lens.

ACKNOWLEDGMENTS

This book is the product of over a decade of research, teaching, and consulting on the nature of innovation success and failure. During this time I have had the incredible good fortune to work with a stunning array of learning partners—my students at Tuck and INSEAD, executives at scores of companies and workshops, and mentors and coauthors in the academic world. They have created the environment, the opportunity, and the impetus to test and refine these ideas in a multitude of settings. I am deeply grateful for their contributions, direct and indirect, to my own understanding and to this undertaking.

In writing the book I have benefited tremendously from the support, advice, and critical feedback of a host of individuals who gave generously of both their time and their insight: Howard Anderson, Julia Batavia, Diane E. Bilotta, Manish Bhandari, Adam Brandenburger, Colin Blaydon, Michael Brimm, Clayton Christensen, Sarah Cliffe, Rudi Coetzee, Dr. Richard J. Comi, Donald Conway, Richard D'Aveni, Yves Doz, Gregg Fairbrothers, Javier Gimeno, Ronny Golan, Vijay Govindarajan, Lars Guldbaek Karlsen, Morten Hansen, Peter Hanson, Hal Hogan, Natalie Horbachevsky, Bob Howell, Barak Hershkovitz, Chris Huston, Chan Kim, Jim Komsa, Kim LaFontana, Karim R. Lakhani, Raphael La Porta, Dan Levinthal, Julien Lévy, Donna McMahon, Halli

Melnitsky, Ashok G. Nachnani, John Owens, Heidy Paust Kelley, Subi Rangan, Lone Reinholdt, Silvija Seres, Todd Shuster, John S. Taylor, Chris Trimble, Bernard Tubiana, Joaquin Villareal, David Wu, Enver Yucesan, and Peter Zemsky. Special thanks go to Rahul Kapoor, my coauthor on the lithography studies that are at the core of Chapter 6, and to the intrepid students in my Research to Practice seminars at Tuck.

I am grateful to Paul Danos and Bob Hansen, Dean and Associate Dean, for creating at the Tuck School an exceptional environment for research and teaching that allowed these ideas to blossom; Syd Finkelstein for support and advice on both macro and micro challenges; Kim Keating for tireless effort and encouragement; Will Vincent for generous counsel and critical input throughout the book-writing process; Steve Stankiewicz for masterfully transforming every exhibit in this book; and Alexia Paul for the invaluable effort, assistance, and insights that were the key to keeping this book on track and on time.

Esmond Harmsworth, agent extraordinaire, was a valued guide and counselor at every stage of the journey. At Portfolio, Adrian Zackheim and Will Weisser were incredibly supportive from the start, and patient and flexible to the end. Brooke Carey, my wonderful editor, was a model of balance and perspective as she helped shape and develop this manuscript.

Greatest thanks go to my family, without whom none of this would matter.

Ron Adner
Hanover, New Hampshire
November 2011

NOTES

[INTRODUCTION]

4   **partners who must work together:** A number of insightful books have been written on the broad topic of business ecosystems. They offer compelling arguments about the importance of considering interdependence. This book complements their insights by offering new structure and tools for addressing ecosystem strategy challenges. Titles include James Moore's *The Death of Competition* (New York: HarperBusiness, 1996); Adam Brandenburger and Barry Nalebuff's *Co-opetition* (New York: Currency Doubleday, 1996); Marco Iansiti and Roy Levien's *The Keystone Advantage* (Boston: Harvard Business School Press, 2004); Annabelle Gawer and Michael Cusumano's *Platform Leadership* (Boston: Harvard Business School Press, 2002); and Henry Chesbrough's *Open Innovation: The New Imperative for Creating and Profiting from Technology* (Boston: Harvard Business School Press, 2005). An early version of the arguments presented in this book appeared in Ron Adner, "Match Your Innovation Strategy to Your Innovation Ecosystem," *Harvard Business Review* 84, no. 4 (April 2006): 98–107.

5   **45 percent fail to meet:** The PDMA data is reported in Abbie Griffin, "PDMA Research on New Product Development Practices: Updating Trends and Benchmarking Best Practices," *Journal of Product Innovation Management* 14 (1997): 429–58. These values are consistent with more recent surveys as reviewed, for example,

in Robert G. Cooper's *Winning at New Products: Creating Value Through Innovation* (New York: Basic Books, 2011).

5   **72 percent of senior executives:** Boston Consulting Group report, "Innovation 2010."

5   **two schools of thought:** All great management books consider multiple facets of the problem but focus on different aspects. Insightful exemplars within the customer-focus school are Clayton Christensen's *The Innovator's Dilemma: When New Technologies Cause Great Firms to Fail* (Boston: Harvard Business School Press, 1997); W. Chan Kim and Renée Mauborgne's *Blue Ocean Strategy* (Boston: Harvard Business School Press, 2004); Geoffrey Moore's *Crossing the Chasm* (New York: HarperBusiness, 1991); George Day's *Market Driven Strategy: Processes for Creating Value* (New York: Free Press, 1999); and J. C. Larachee's *The Momentum Effect* (Upper Saddle River, NJ: Prentice Hall, 2008). Exemplars of the implementation school are Jim Collins's *Good to Great* (New York: HarperBusiness, 2001); Larry Bossidy and Ram Charan's *Execution* (New York: Crown Business, 2002); Jack and Suzy Welch's *Winning* (New York: HarperBusiness, 2005); Sydney Finkelstein's *Why Smart Executives Fail* (New York: Portfolio, 2003); and Vijay Govindarajan and Chris Trimble's *Other Side of Innovation* (Boston: Harvard Business Review Press, 2010).

9   **2011 survey:** Corporate Executive Board, "Building a Culture of Innovation," 2011.

[CHAPTER 1]

17   **"The PAX System is our biggest technological breakthrough":** "Michelin PAX System," Michelin.com, http://www.michelinman.com/pax/. Accessed September 16, 2010.

17   **"we have reinvented the tire":** Chris Vander Doelen, "Run-Flats Give Tires an Inflated Value," *National Post* (Canada), November 12, 2004.

17   **"The adoption of the PAX System is inevitable":** Comments made at "Huitièmes Journées d'Histoire," conference at l'ecole de Paris du

management, March 22, 2002, transcript page 30, www.anrt.asso
.fr/fr/pdf/CRateliers2002.pdf.

17 **"most important component on a vehicle":** "Tire Basics: Getting
a Grip on Tire Fundamentals," *Motor Trend,* April 2005.

19 **flat tires were both prevalent . . . and dangerous:** Tire Safety Survey conducted for the AAA Foundation for Traffic Safety by Roper
Starch Worldwide Inc., March 22, 1999, http://www.aaafoundation
.org/pdf/tss.pdf.

19 **"a major development in vehicle safety":** Warren Brown, "From
Michelin, a Pricey New Tire That Survives Blowouts," *Washington
Post,* October 24, 2004.

22 **"Goodyear and Michelin are convinced . . . PAX System is the
best":** "Michelin, Goodyear in Run-Flat Tyre Venture," Reuters,
June 23, 2000.

22 **seven out of eight consumers chose run-flats:** Brad Dawson, "Tire
Maker Eyes High-Profit, High-Tech Mix in '02," *Rubber & Plastics
News,* February 25, 2002.

23 **"They perform better in every respect":** William Diem, "Michelin's
Pax System Gaining Momentum," *Rubber & Plastics News,* March
22, 1999.

23 **by 2010 more than 80 percent of cars would be fitted with run-
flats:** David Shaw, "BMW Dominates Runflat Tyres as PAX Goes
Down," *European Rubber Journal,* May 1, 2005.

23 **"The bottom-line benefit for the customers":** Leslie Allen, "Michelin
Rolls Out New Run-Flat Design," *Chicago Tribune,* February 11, 2005.

23 **"traditional service and repair networks will continue to grow":**
"Michelin PAX System Innovations Extend to Customer Service," *PR
Newswire,* September 27, 2004, http://www.prnewswire.com/news-
releases/michelinr-pax-systemtm-innovations-extend-to-customer
-service-73940867.html. Accessed October 4, 2010.

24 **several class-action lawsuits were filed:** Kathy McCarron, "Running Away from Run-Flats," *Tire Business,* March 26, 2007.

24 **"we do not intend to develop a new PAX":** David Shaw, "Michelin: No Push for PAX," *Rubber & Plastics News,* November 26, 2007.

25 **"not unlike the transition to radial from bias":** Vera Fedchenko, "Run-Flat Revolution Gaining Ground in OE," *Rubber & Plastics News,* October 31, 2005.

30 **installing an air pressure monitor:** Federal Motor Vehicle Safety Standards: Tire Pressure Monitoring Systems; Controls and Displays, Department of Transportation, NHTSA, http://www.nhtsa .gov/cars/rules/rulings/TirePressure/fedreg.htm. Accessed October 3, 2010.

30 **the window of opportunity:** The 2000 Transportation Recall Enhancement Accountability Documentation (TREAD) Act in the U.S. Congress. Drawn up in the wake of the Firestone tire recall on Ford Explorers, the TREAD Act mandated that by 2007 all new cars come equipped with a tire pressure monitoring system (TPMS). Michelin, J.D. Powers, and all the other industry participants were well aware of the act when making their heroic predictions of PAX success as late as 2004 in the expectation that PAX would become the standard before the act went into effect— more evidence of an industry blind spot.

32 **over 3,500 Strykers have been built:** "General Dynamics Awarded Contract for Stryker Production," *Deagel.com,* October 9, 2009, http://www.deagel.com/news/General-Dynamics-Awarded-Contract-for-Stryker-Production_n000006659.aspx. Accessed October 18, 2010.

[CHAPTER 2]

40 **by the year 2000, mobile network operators had over 700 million users:** "Free Statistics: Mobile Cellular Subscriptions," International Telecommunication Union, http://www.itu.int/ITU-D/ ict/statistics/.

40 **70 percent of adults had a mobile phone:** "The Winners' Curse," *Economist,* June 14, 2001, http://www.economist.com/node/657390.

41 **"next stage in the growth of the communications business":** Niall McKay, "Amid Telecommunications Gloom, Optimism in France," *New York Times,* February 23, 2001.

41 **"we do not know what services will eventually emerge for 3G":** Peter Lewis, "State of the Art Heading North to the Wireless Future," *New York Times,* June 1, 2000.

41 **3G business would match the size of Ericsson's 2G:** Paul Tate, "Mobile: Going Thataway," *ZDNet.com,* December 10, 2000, http://www.zdnetasia.com/mobile-going-thataway-21163436.htm.

41 **handset makers could sell everyone new phones:** "Nokia succumbs," *Economist,* June 14, 2001, http://www.economist.com/node/656251.

41 **"two of the fastest-growing technologies of all time":** "Waves of the Future," *Economist,* July 6, 2000, http://www.economist.com/node/4937.

42 **$175 billion to build out their networks:** "The Winners' Curse," *Economist,* June 14, 2001.

42 **Nokia had been working on 3G prototypes:** Stephen Baker, "3G's Latest Snafu: Hellacious Handsets," *BusinessWeek,* November 26, 2001, http://www.businessweek.com/magazine/content/01_48_/b3759154.htm.

43 **"the most complex consumer electronics devices ever designed":** Ibid.

43 **actual number was closer to 3 million:** "Insight: Nokia Business Review 2000," annual report, 2001.

50 **increasing the chances of success to 16 percent:** 0.85 × 0.85 × 0.75 × 0.3 = 0.1626.

52 **"the battle of devices has now become a war of ecosystems":** "Full Text: Nokia CEO Stephen Elop's 'Burning Platform' Memo," *Wall Street Journal,* February 9, 2011, http://blogs.wsj.com/tech-europe/2011/02/09/full-text-nokia-ceo-stephen-elops-burning-platform-memo/.

53 **$2.5 billion write-down:** Martin Du Bois and Richard Hudson, "Philips Confirms Severe Troubles in Its Consumer Electronics Business," *Wall Street Journal Europe,* August 7, 1992, p. 3.

[CHAPTER 3]

56 **"most significant improvements to the products in more than a decade":** Microsoft, "2007 Microsoft Office System Is Golden," press release, November 6, 2006, http://www.microsoft.com/presspass/press/2006/nov06/11-062007OfficeRTMPR.mspx.

58 **revenues of close to $4 billion:** Leonard Pukaite, "The Hard Truth," *Cutting Tool Engineering,* June 1996.

60 **15 percent of the abrasives market:** "Freedonia Focus on Abrasives," Freedonia Group Inc., October 2010, p. 6.

60 **staff needed to be retrained:** J. F. G. Oliveira, E. J. Silva, C. Guo, F. Hashimoto, "Industrial Challenges in Grinding," *CIRP Annals— Manufacturing Technology,* January 2009, p. 665.

60 **most of the market opted to stay with traditional grinding wheels:** Ibid.

66 **first commercial DLP . . . projectors:** "DLP History," Texas Instruments DLP Web site, DLP.com, 2009, http://www.dlp.com/technology/dlp-history/default.aspx.

67 **development of the digital telecine scanner:** Kevin Shaw, "A Brief History for Colorists," Finalcolor.com, May 23, 2010, http://www.finalcolor.com/history4colorists.htm.

67 *Star Wars: Episode I—Phantom Menace* **was screened:** "DLP History," DLP.com.

67 **40 percent by the end of 2010:** "MPAA Theatrical Market Statistics," Motion Picture Association of America, 2010, http://www.mpaa.org/Resources/93bbeb16-0e4d-4b7e-b085-3f41c459f9ac.pdf.

68 **avoiding the $1 billion spent annually:** Charles S. Swartz, *Understanding Digital Cinema: A Professional Handbook* (Focal Press, 2004).

68 **studio's printing cost alone can come to $7.5 million:** Sherman Fridman, "Theaters to Convert to Digital Movies," *Newsbytes,* May 30, 2000.

68 **Traditionally, movies were rolled out in a staggered fashion:** Katherine Monk, "Thwarting the Pirates: Sony Hopes Global Release Strategy Will Take a Bite Out of Illegal File Sharing," *National Post* (Canada), May 18, 2006.

68 **alternative to pirated films:** Ibid.

68 **digital film technology allowed for encryption:** Ibid.

69 **"Digital cinema is like looking out of a window":** Ann Donahue, "Paving the Way for Digital Projection," *Variety,* March 7, 2001.

69 **$70,000–$100,000 per screen conversion cost:** Nicole Norfleet, "Theaters Weigh Pros and Cons of 3D Conversion," *Washington Post,* April 19, 2010.

69 **digital projectors have a life span of only ten years:** MKPE Consulting, "Digital Cinema Business: Frequently Asked Questions," September 2010, www.mkpe.com/digital_cinema/faqs/.

70 **"It's up to exhibitors, now":** "James Cameron Keynote NAB2006 Digital Cinema Summit," DV.com, March 2, 2006, http://www.dv .com/article/22026.

70 **"we'll be out of business":** Ty Burr, "Reel Gone? Why Are Multiplex Owners Afraid to Byte?," *EW.com,* May 7, 2001, http://www .ew.com/ew/article/0,108459,00.html.

70 **came together to form Digital Cinema Initiatives:** Digital Cinema Initiatives LLC, 2011, www.dcimovies.com.

71 **"if we left it up to the exhibitor":** Carl DiOrio, "Studios Near D-Day," *Variety,* March 25, 2002.

71 **"a little longer than people had expected":** Carl DiOrio, "D-Cinema Systems on Hold As Studios Set Standards," *Variety,* February 3, 2003.

71 **theater owners were unwilling:** MKPE Consulting, "Digital Cinema Business."

72 **"have their act together this year, or it'll fall apart":** David Lieberman, "Digital Film Revolution Poised to Start Rolling," *USA Today*, May 18, 2005.

72 **"The proportion of financing":** Eric Taub, "Questions of Cost Greet New Digital Projectors," *International Herald Tribune,* June 2, 2004.

72 **whatever form the financing plan took, it must be industry-wide:** Gabriel Snyder, "NATO Takes Digital Stand," *Variety*, November 22, 2004.

73 **80 percent of the exhibitor's conversion costs:** "The VPF Model," Arts Alliance Media, http://www.artsalliancemedia.com/vpf/.

74 **James Cameron's 3-D record-breaking sci-fi megahit:** Brandon Gray, "'Avatar' Claims Highest Gross of All Time," BoxOffice Mojo.com, February 3, 2010.

74 *Toy Story 3* **became 2010's top-grossing picture:** David Twiddy, "Theaters Will Add Dimension with Digital Systems Upgrade," *Kansas City Business Journal*, March 28, 2010.

74 **38 percent of U.S. screens:** David Hancock, "Digital Screen Numbers and Forecasts to 2015 Are Finalised," *Screen Digest*, January 26, 2011.

74 **The costs of digital preservation:** A fascinating discussion can be found in *The Digital Dilemma: Strategic Issues in Archiving and Accessing Digital Motion Picture Materials*, Science and Technology Council of the Academy of Motion Picture Arts and Sciences, 2007.

[CHAPTER 4]

84 **value chains and supply chains:** Classic books on value chains include Michael Porter's *Competitive Advantage* (New York: Free Press, 1998) and Charles Fine's *Clockspeed* (New York: Perseus Books, 1998). Adam Brandenburger and Barry Nalebuff introduce the role of complementors in *Co-opetition* (New York: Currency, 1996), and Clayton

Christensen discusses the roles of value networks in affecting innovation incentives in *The Innovator's Dilemma* (Boston: Harvard Business School Press, 1997). The value blueprint builds on these perspectives, with a focus on designing the most effective configuration to deliver the value proposition.

88 **$550 device:** "Sony Shows Data Discman," *New York Times,* September 13, 1991.

88 **The Rocket, developed by NuvoMedia:** Martin Arnold, "From Gutenberg to Cyberstories," *New York Times,* January 7, 1999.

88 **That same year the SoftBook:** Peter Lewis, "Taking on New Forms, Electronic Books Turn a Page," *New York Times,* July 2, 1998.

88 **Gemstar released two models:** Ken Feinstein, "RCA REB1100 eBook Review," *CNET.com,* February 21, 2001, http://reviews.cnet.com/e-book-readers/rca-reb1100-ebook/4505-3508_7-4744438.html.

89 **proof that the electronic book was ready for the mainstream:** Doreen Carvajal, "Long Line Online for Stephen King E-Novella," *New York Times,* March 16, 2000.

90 **Random House's e-book revenues doubled:** Nicholas Bogaty, "eBooks by the Numbers: Open eBook Forum Compiles Industry Growth Stats," International Digital Publishing Forum, press release, July 22, 2002, http://old.idpf.org/pressroom/pressreleases/ebookstats.htm.

90 **"difficult to find, buy and read e-books":** Steven Levy, "The Future of Reading," *Newsweek,* November 26, 2007.

90 **Paltry content and intense digital rights management:** Ginny Parker Woods, "Sony Cracks Open New Book with Reader," *Toronto Star,* February 20, 2006.

90 **"We've been very cautious in launching [the Reader]":** Michael Kanellos, "Sony's Brave Sir Howard," *CNET.com,* January 17, 2007, http://news.cnet.com/Sonys-brave-Sir-Howard/2008-1041_3-6150661.html.

90   **almost 20 percent cheaper than the Librié:** Sony Librié ebook Review, *eReaderGuide.Info,* www.ereaderguide.info/sony_librie_ ebook_reader_review.htm.

90   **10,000 titles available at Connect.com:** Edward Baig, "Sony Device Gets E-Book Smart," *USA Today,* October 5, 2006.

91   **the iPod of the book industry:** David Derbyshire, "Electronic Book Opens New Chapter for Readers," *Daily Telegraph,* September 28, 2006.

91   **much fanfare from the press:** Amanda Andrews, "Sony's Hitting the Books," *Australian,* February 28, 2006.

92   **lowering publisher confidence:** George Cole, "Will the eBook Finally Replace Paper?," *Guardian,* October 5, 2006.

93   **"four factors need to be in place":** Ibid.

93   **Barnes & Noble superstore carries as many as 200,000 titles:** Barnes & Noble company profile, Hoover's Inc., Hoovers.com.

94   **backlist titles went for as low as $4:** Charles McGrath, "Can't Judge an E-Book by Its Screen? Well, Maybe You Can," *New York Times,* November 24, 2006.

94   **difference between the cost:** Peter Wayner, "An Entire Bookshelf, in Your Hands," *New York Times,* August 9, 2007.

96   **"downright industrially ugly":** Tom Regan, "Costly 'Kindle' Reader Gets a Lot of It Right," *Christian Science Monitor,* November 28, 2007, http://www.csmonitor.com/2007/1127/p25s01-stct.html.

96   **weighed more, and had an inferior screen:** Product specs (4-shade gray scale vs. 8), Amazon.com, http://www.amazon.com/Kindle-Amazons-Original-Wireless-generation/dp/B000FI73MA/ref=cm_cr_pr_product_top.

96   **"This isn't a device, it's a service":** Levy, "The Future of Reading."

96   **330,000 within two years:** Motoko Rich, "Barnes & Noble Jumps into E-Book Sales with Both Feet," *International Herald Tribune,* July 22, 2009.

97   **$9.99 or less:** David Pogue, "Books Pop Up, Wirelessly," *New York Times,* November 22, 2007.

97 **"works as a stand-alone device":** "A Conversation with Amazon
.com CEO Jeff Bezos," *Charlie Rose,* November 19, 2007.

97 **"King of the Retail Jungle":** Farhad Manjoo, "Amazon, King of
the Retail Jungle," *Washington Post,* February 8, 2009.

97 **30 percent of books sold in the United States:** "40: Jeff Bezos—CEO,
Amazon.com [The Global Elite]," *Newsweek,* December 19, 2008,
http://www.thedailybeast.com/newsweek/2008/12/19/40-jeff
-bezos.html.

97 **Kindle was both closed and proprietary:** Rob Pegoraro, "Kin-
dled, but Not Enlightened," *Washington Post,* December 6, 2007.

98 **Amazon sacrificed some e-book profits up-front:** David Gelles
and Andrew Edgecliffe-Johnson, "A Page Is Turned," *Financial
Times,* February 9, 2010.

98 **able to make up much of the difference:** Mark Muro, "The New
Republic: The Kindle, America's Decline," *NPR.org,* February 26,
2010, http://www.npr.org/templates/story/story.php?storyId=124
107775.

98 **margins of $200 per unit:** "Major Cost Drivers in the Amazon
Kindle 2," iSuppli Corporation, April 2009.

98 **at the behest of publishers:** Motoko Rich and Brad Stone, "Publisher Wins Fight with Amazon over E-Books," *New York Times,*
January 31, 2010, http://www.nytimes.com/2010/02/01/technology
/companies/01amazonweb.html.

99 **$3 billion on e-books:** James McQuivey, "eBook Buying Is About
to Spiral Upward: U.S. eBook Forecast, 2010 to 2015," Forrester
Research, November 5, 2010.

99 **e-book sales were fast approaching $120 million:** Industry Statis-
tics, International Digital Publishing Forum, 2011, http://idpf
.org/about-us/industry-statistics#Additional_Global_eBook
_Sales_Figures.

99 **it held 80 percent market share:** Gelles and Edgecliffe-Johnson,
"A Page Is Turned."

99   **estimated sales of the Kindle at 6 million:** Sam Gustin, "Amazon Says New Kindle Is Its Top-Selling Product," *Wired,* December 27, 2010.

99   **48 percent market share of e-readers:** IDC, "Nearly 18 Million Media Tablets Shipped in 2010 with Apple Capturing 83% Share; eReader Shipments Quadrupled to More Than 12 Million, According to IDC," press release, March 10, 2011.

100 **fighting to hold the number five spot:** Ibid.

101 **347 million diabetics worldwide:** Goodarz Danaei et al., "National, Regional, and Global Trends in Fasting Plasma Glucose and Diabetes Prevalence Since 1980: Systematic Analysis of Health Examination Surveys and Epidemiological Studies with 370 Country-Years and 2.7 Million Participants," *Lancet* 378, no. 9785 (July 2, 2011): 31–40.

101 **25 million diabetics in the United States:** "National Diabetes Statistics, 2011," National Diabetes Information Clearinghouse, National Institute of Diabetes and Digestive and Kidney Diseases of the National Institutes of Health, http://diabetes.niddk.nih .gov/DM/PUBS/statistics/.

101 **"We've never had such a response":** Laurie Barclay, "Exubera Approved Despite Initial Lung Function Concerns," Medscape Medical News, *WebMD,* February 9, 2006.

102 **annual costs of diabetes in the United States alone is over $200 billion:** Diabetes Statistics, American Diabetes Association, January 26, 2011, citing a 2007 study. Note that medical costs have risen substantially since then, so this is a very conservative estimate.

102 **"These products, if approved, could expand the market for insulin":** "New Formulations Set to Transform Diabetes Treatment," *In-PharmaTechnologist.com,* June 16, 2003.

102 **sales of more than $1.5 billion by 2009:** Morgan Stanley Dean Witter Equity Research, North America, "Pfizer Inc.—Rational Exuberance?," May 7, 2001.

102 **device would garner $1 billion annually by 2007:** Credit Suisse First Boston Equity Research, "Pfizer—Confirms European Filing of Exubera," March 4, 2004.

102 **"breakthrough medical advance":** Peter Brandt, Pfizer Q2 2006 earnings conference call, July 20, 2006, p. 3.

102 **"Pfizer will have a blockbuster product on its hands":** Val Brickates Kennedy, "Firms to Vie for Inhaled-Insulin Sales," *Market-Watch*, May 7, 2005, http://www.marketwatch.com/story/drug -rivals-to-vie-for-share-of-inhaled-insulin-market.

103 **buy out Aventis's share in Exubera for $1.3 billion:** "Pfizer to Acquire Global Rights to an Insulin That Is Inhaled," *New York Times*, January 13, 2006.

104 **"a wealth of experience with not just the use of insulin":** Brandt, Pfizer conference call, p. 16.

105 **estimated $1.5 billion in Exubera sales by 2010:** Morgan Stanley, "Pfizer," equity research report, February 12, 2006; Bear Stearns, "Pfizer—Enthusiasm Building Ahead of Exubera Launch," equity research report, June 12, 2006.

105 **projecting "only" $1.3 billion:** West LB Equity Research, "Novo Nordisk," equity research report, November 8, 2006.

106 **launched its "full-court press":** "Kindler's Honeymoon Over? Analysts Press Pfizer Execs on Series of Stumbles," *Pink Sheet*, April 1, 2007.

106 **would reach $2 billion, although perhaps not by 2010:** "Pfizer Plans Exubera 'Full Court Press' in 2007 after 2006 Stumbles," *Pink Sheet*, January 29, 2007.

106 **sales "continued to be disappointing":** Cathy Dombrowski, "Lilly Expects Experience to Help Avoid Mistakes of Pfizer's Exubera Launch," *Pink Sheet*, September 1, 2007.

106 **Exubera was dead:** "As Pfizer Closes Door on Exubera, Has Window Opened for Others?," *Pink Sheet*, October 22, 2007.

106 **"one of the most stunning failures"**: Avery Johnson, "Insulin Flop Costs Pfizer $2.8 Billion," *Wall Street Journal,* October 19, 2007. Quote is from Mike Krensavage, an analyst at Raymond James & Associates.

107 **"it was kind of like generation zero"**: "As Pfizer Closes Door on Exubera, Has Window Opened for Others?"

107 **"doesn't diminish our enthusiasm for our product"**: Lilly Q3 2007 earnings conference call, October 18, 2007, p. 12.

107 **Pfizer wrote off $2.8 billion:** Johnson, "Insulin Flop Costs Pfizer." Lilly's write-off was reported in its Q1 2009 results. Novo's charge of 1.3 billion Danish kroner ($260 million) was reported in its financial statement for 2007, issued January 31, 2008.

108 **some patients would embrace the inhaler, while others would balk:** There are scores of positive testimonials as well as heartbreaking pleas by patients on Exubera urging Pfizer not to pull the drug. Online discussion boards are rife with back-and-forth debates between patients who loved Exubera and skeptics who criticized (but usually hadn't tried) it. The following quote from reader comments to a *BusinessWeek* article on Exubera, posted October 26, 2007, captures the typical sentiment of Exubera's supporters : "After multiple daily insulin injections since 1974, I have finally been given an insulin delivery system that works beautifully. . . . This delivery system works perfectly as touted. Cumbersome, BIG Deal! As if taking injections doesn't command stares and comments in public. For years I went to the restrooms for injections in public . . . now there is a sanitary place. Exubera was my dream come true."

109 **"target those highly experienced, primarily endocrinologists"**: Peter Brandt, Pfizer Q2 2006 earnings conference call, July 20, 2006, p. 12.

109 **"we don't see that as an issue"**: Ibid, p. 20.

111 **endocrinologists were so overbooked:** Andrew F. Stewart, "The United States Endocrinology Workforce: A Supply-Demand Mismatch," *Journal of Clinincal Endocrinology & Metabolism* 93, no. 4 (April 2008): 1164–66.

112 **has spent nearly $1 billion of founder Alfred Mann's own money:**
David Holley, "MannKind Stock Plummets After FDA Rejects
Insulin Inhalant," *Daily Deal,* January 21, 2011.

112 **MedTone device was one-tenth the size of the bulky Exubera:**
Ibid.

112 **Technosphere Insulin System closely mimics the release of insulin:** "Type 1 Diabetes: MannKind Initiates Two U.S. Pivotal Phase
III Studies of Inhaled Technosphere Insulin," *Drug Week,* April
7, 2006.

112 **company is "certainly resolved to pursue":** MannKind Q4 2010
earnings conference call, February 10, 2011.

[CHAPTER 5]

119 **number to be as high as 98,000:** Linda Kohn, Janet Corrigan, and
Molla Donaldson, eds., *To Err Is Human: Building a Safer Health
System* (Washington, DC: Institute of Medicine National Academy
Press, 1999).

119 **adverse events occur in one-third of hospital admissions:** David
C. Classen et al., "'Global Trigger Tool' Shows That Adverse
Events in Hospitals May Be Ten Times Greater Than Previously
Measured," *Health Affairs* 30, no. 4 (April 2011): 581–89.

119 **still in place in approximately 80 percent of American hospitals:**
Lena Sun, "Doctors Wary of Switch to Digital Records," *Washington Post,* March 15, 2011.

119 **drug errors alone are estimated to harm 1.5 million people per
year:** Gardiner Harris, "Report Finds a Heavy Toll from Medication Errors," *New York Times,* July 21, 2006.

119 **"solutions to medical mistakes will ultimately come through better information technology":** Robert Wachter, "The End of the
Beginning: Patient Safety Five Years After 'To Err Is Human,'"
Health Affairs, November 30, 2004, http://content.healthaffairs
.org/content/suppl/2004/11/29/hlthaff.w4.534.DC1.

119 **a $2 trillion industry:** David Ahern, introductory remarks presented at a seminar entitled "Patient-Centered Computing and e-Health: Transforming Healthcare Quality," Boston, Mass., March 29, 2008.

119 **health-care industry spends only 2 percent:** "The No-Computer Virus—IT in the Health-Care Industry," *Economist* 375, no. 8424 (April 30, 2005): 72.

119 **gain of nearly 30 percent efficiency:** Steve Lohr, "Who Pays for Efficiency?," *New York Times,* June 11, 2007.

120 **more than 20,000 forms each year:** TelecomWorldWire, "IBM Heads Venture for Electronic Health Records," *M2 Communications,* December 5, 2005.

120 **"safety savings of $142–$371 billion":** Richard Hillestad et al., "Can Electronic Medical Record Systems Transform Health Care? Potential Health Benefits, Savings, and Costs," *Health Affairs* 24, no. 5 (2005): 1103–17, http://content.healthaffairs.org/content/24/5/1103.abstract.

120 **devoted massive resources:** Larry Pawola, "The History of the Electronic Health Record," University of Illinois at Chicago HIMSS (Healthcare Information and Management Systems Society) 2011 Conference, Orlando, Fla., February 22, 2011.

121 **more than 5,000 pharmacies by 1997:** "IBM & Medic Computer Online Prescription Deal," *Newsbytes,* February 24, 1997.

121 **Health Data Network Express, announced in 1998:** Steve Shipside, "Nurse, the Screens," *Guardian,* March 26, 1998.

121 **IBM teamed up with several providers:** Doug Bartholomew, "Health Care's Shocking Affliction: This Trillion-Dollar Industry Is Shamefully Backward When It Comes to IT," *Industry Week,* August 2002.

121 **an HMO with nearly 9 million members:** Marianne Kolbasuk McGee, "IBM, Geisinger Health Deal Aims to Provide More Personalized Patient Care," *InformationWeek,* October 11, 2006.

121 **Dossia, an employer-led program:** Marianne Kolbasuk McGee, "Another E-Health Project in Disarray," *InformationWeek*, July 14, 2007.

121 **"It's time to modernize the health care system":** Julie Appleby, "Tech Executives Push for Digital Medical Records," *USA Today*, October 13, 2005.

122 **HealthVault, a free Web-based health records system:** Marianne Kolbasuk McGee, "Microsoft Unveils Free Web Health Tools for Consumers," *InformationWeek*, October 4, 2007.

122 **as late as 2009 only 9 percent of U.S. hospitals had implemented:** Walecia Konrad, "Some Caveats About Keeping Your Own Electronic Health Records," *New York Times*, April 18, 2009.

124 **hefty sales price ($20 to $50 million):** Rainu Kaushal et al., "The Costs of a National Health Information Network," *Annals of Internal Medicine* 143, no. 3 (August 2005): 165–73.

124 **kill more than 90,000 patients per year globally:** Pauline Chen, M.D., "Why Don't Doctors Wash Their Hands More?," *New York Times*, September 17, 2009.

125 **"instead of investing in that, many hospitals are out building new buildings":** Jennifer Steinhauer, "A Health Revolution, in Baby Steps," *New York Times*, October 15, 2000.

125 **The Mayo Clinic, University of Pittsburgh Medical Center:** Steve Lohr, "Most Doctors Aren't Using Electronic Health Records," *New York Times*, June 19, 2008.

126 **handoffs among departments are streamlined:** Richard Quinn, "Digital Dilemma: HM Groups Need a Proactive Approach to Health Technology Design and Implementation," *Hospitalist*, September 2009.

127 **improved quality of life:** The development of the electronic picture archiving and communication system (PACS) in the 1980s furthered the adoption of EHR in radiology. PACS allows X-ray or CAT scan images to be transmitted digitally, eliminating the cost

of printing and storing hard copies. The system also allows radiologists to record their interpretations. Traditionally, findings would be dictated into a recording device such as a Dictaphone. With PACS, radiologists rely on voice recognition software to transcribe their findings, another example of why radiology's transition to EHR was relatively uncontroversial.

These departments are more than early adopters—they are pre-adopter, typically having put in their department-specific systems years before the administration started moving toward hospital-wide EHR. So while they are most ready to appreciate the benefits of digital, they are often loath to give up their existing systems, which are often not compatible with hospital-wide solutions. This makes them highly imperfect allies in the quest to extend the seamless EHR footprint across departments.

127 **78 percent of hospitals were enabled with electronic radiology:** A. K. Jha et al., "Use of Electronic Health Records in U.S. Hospitals," *New England Journal of Medicine* 360, no. 16 (April 2009): 1628–38.

127 **doctor productivity dipping 20 percent:** Julie Schmit, "Health Care's Paper Trail Is Costly Route," *USA Today,* July 20, 2004.

129 **total of 3.9 billion prescriptions filled:** "Prescription Drug Trends," Kaiser Family Foundation, May 2010, http://www.kff .org/rxdrugs/upload/3057-08.pdf.

130 **"We underestimated the challenges":** Marianne Kolbasuk McGee, "Intel, Wal-Mart, and Others Refocus to Get Worker E-Health Record System Running," *InformationWeek,* September 17, 2007.

131 **serving over 8.5 million veterans at 1,100 facilities:** "Largest U.S. Health Care System Links Staff and Resources," Esri.com, Fall 2010, http://www.esri.com/news/arcnews/fall10articles/largest-us -health.html.

131 **VHA has an error rate of just 0.003 percent:** Catherine Arnst, "The Best Medical Care in the U.S.," *BusinessWeek,* July 17, 2006.

131 **allocated substantial funding ($27 billion):** Steve Lohr, "Carrots, Sticks and Digital Health Records," *New York Times,* February 27, 2011.

131 **prior administration's $50 million:** Julia Adler-Milstein and David Bates, "Paperless Healthcare: Progress and Challenges of an IT-Enabled Healthcare System," *Business Horizons* 53, no. 2 (March–April 2010): 119–30.

131 **"meaningful use of certified EHR systems":** David Blumenthal, "Stimulating the Adoption of Healthcare Information Technology," *New England Journal of Medicine* 360, no. 15 (April 2009): 1477–79.

131 **receive up to $44,000:** Lena Sun, "Doctors Wary of Switch to Digital Records," *Washington Post,* March 15, 2011.

131 **in 2015, these carrots turn to sticks:** Blumenthal, "Stimulating the Adoption of Health Information Technology."

131 **updating digital records with diagnoses, monitoring drug interactions:** *Washington Post,* March 15, 2011.

135 **cutting the follower out of the ecosystem:** The book *Platform Leadership* by Gawer and Cusumano offers an interesting exploration of this issue from the perspective of the leader. See also *The Keystone Advantage* by Iansiti and Levien.

[CHAPTER 6]

141 **Sony's Walkman retained a 50 percent market share:** Susan Sanderson and Mustafa Uzumeri, "Managing Product Families: The Case of Sony Walkman," *Research Policy* 24, no.5 (April 1994), pp. 762–63.

142 **increase capacity to a then unheard-of 6 GB:** Eliot Van Buskirk, "Bragging Rights to the World's First MP3 Player," *CNET.com,* January 25, 2005, http://news.cnet.com/Bragging-rights-to-the-worlds-first-MP3-player/2010-1041_3-5548180.html.

142 **unit sales in 2001 were only 248,000:** Hong Kong Trade Development Council, "MP3 Jukebox Has US Sales Rocking and Rolling," *Hong Kong Trader,* June 25, 2002, http://www.hktdc.com/info/vp/a/ict/en/1/2/1/1X00G4BD/MP3-Jukebox-Has-US-Sales-Rocking-And-Rolling.htm.

143 **"they'll never go back to dial-up":** Sylvia Dennis, "High Speed Net Access Market to Reach 16Mil US Households," *Newsbytes,* September 1, 1998.

143 **"cumbersome to move even compressed CDs around":** Doug Reece, "Industry Grapples with MP3 Dilemma," *Billboard,* July 18, 1998.

144 **"Apple has about 5 percent market share":** Joe Wilcox, "25 Apple Stores to Sprout This Year," *CNET.com,* May 15, 2001, http://news .cnet.com/25-Apple-stores-to-sprout-this-year/2100-1040_3 -257633.html.

144 **"I am going to wait for the next big thing":** Quoted in Richard Rumelt, *Good Strategy/Bad Strategy: The Difference and Why It Matters* (New York: Crown Business, 2011), p. 14.

145 **"things are slowing down in the MP3 player market":** Peter Brown, "Is MP3 Here to Stay?," *EDN.com,* June 25, 2001, http:// www.edn.com/article/484332-Is_MP3_Here_to_Stay_.php.

145 **"the hit of the holiday season":** Arik Hesseldahl, "iPod's a Winner," *Forbes.com,* December 7, 2001, http://www.forbes.com/2001/ 12/07/1207tentech.html.

145 **"revolutionary," and "brilliant":** Eliot Van Buskirk, "How the iPod Will Change Computing," *CNET.com,* November 2, 2001, http://reviews.cnet.com/4520-6450_7-5020659-1.html.

146 **purchased over 600,000 iPods:** "Apple Press Info," Apple.com., 2011, http://www.apple.com/pr/products/ipodhistory/. Accessed July 23, 2011.

146 **Apple held only 15 percent of the digital player market:** Brian Garrity, "Digital Devices Get Smaller, Capacity Grows; Will Consumers Respond?," *Billboard,* November 9, 2002.

146 **"iTunes Music Store offers a groundbreaking solution":** Apple, "Apple Launches the iTunes Music Store," press release, April 28, 2003.

146 **200,000 songs from major labels:** Ibid.

146 **8 billion songs:** William Blair & Company, "Apple Inc.," equity research report, September 2, 2009.

146 **operating margin of 10 percent:** Estimate from report by Pacific Crest Securities analyst Andy Hargreaves, discussed in Eric Savitz, "Apple: Turns Out, iTunes Makes Money, Pacific Crest Says, Subscription Service Seems Inevitable," *Tech Trader Daily*, April 23, 2007.

146 **compatible with both FireWire and USB cables:** Michelle Megna, "Apple's Shining Moment: The Company Hits the Right Notes with Its New Online Music Store and Revamped iPods," New York *Daily News*, May 11, 2003.

146 **sales of portable CD players were still more than double:** Christopher Walsh, "All They Want for Xmas Is the iPod," *Billboard*, January 29, 2005.

147 **sales of the iPod had leaped 616 percent:** Mark Evans, "Apple's iPod Is 'the Kleenex' of MP3 Players: Cultural Phenomenon Garnered Apple US$1.1-Billion in Q3," *National Post* (Canada), July 15, 2005.

147 **closest competitor with 8 percent market share:** IDC data cited in William Blair & Company, "Apple Inc.," equity research report., September 2, 2009.

147 **"These waves of technology, you can see them way before they happen":** Betsy Morris, "Steve Jobs Speaks Out," *Fortune*, March 7, 2008.

147 **"the Walkman of the early 21st century":** "Behind the Smiles at Sony," *Economist*, March 12, 2005.

148 **pioneers are the ones with arrows in their backs:** Peter N. Golder and Gerard J. Tellis, "Pioneer Advantage: Marketing Logic or Marketing Legend?," *Journal of Marketing Research* 30, no. 2 (May 1993): 158–70; Subramanian Rangan and Ron Adner, "Profits and the Internet: Seven Misconceptions," *MIT Sloan Management Review* 42, no. 4 (Summer 2001): 44–53; and Marvin B. Lieberman and David B. Montgomery, "First-Mover (Dis)advantages: Retrospec-

tive and Link with the Resource-Based View," *Strategic Management Journal* 19, no. 12 (1998): 1111–25.

150 **four-year project focused on the semiconductor lithography industry:** Rahul Kapoor and Ron Adner, "Managing Transitions in the Semiconductor Lithography Ecosystem," *Solid State Technology (50th Anniversary Perspectives Issue),* November 2007, offers a brief primer on the history of lithography. For the full study on early-mover advantage, see Adner and Kapoor, "Value Creation in Innovation Ecosystems: How the Structure of Technological Interdependence Affects Firm Performance in New Technology Generations," *Strategic Management Journal* 31 (2010): 306–333. A second study, Adner and Kapoor, "Innovation Ecosystems and the Pace of Substitution: Re-examining Technology S-curves," 2011, examines broad patterns of technology substitution in the industry (Tuck School working paper).

[CHAPTER 7]

166 **largest car manufacturer in the United States:** David Kirsch, *The Electric Vehicle and the Burden of History* (New Brunswick, N.J.: Rutgers University Press, 2000), p. 31.

166 **"electric vehicle industry is well established":** Ibid., p. 29.

166 **99 percent of these contained gasoline-burning internal combustion engines:** Ibid., p. 15.

166 **GM's unveiling of the Impact:** Seth Fletcher, *Bottled Lightning: Superbatteries, Electric Cars, and the New Lithium Economy* (New York: Hill and Wang, 2011), p. 80.

167 **between $399 and $549 per month:** Keith Naughton, "Detroit: It Isn't Easy Going Green," *BusinessWeek* (international edition), December 15, 1997.

167 **approximately 1 billion vehicles:** Deborah Gordon and Daniel Sperling, "Surviving Two Billion Cars: China Must Lead the Way," *Yale Environment* 360, March 5, 2009; see also "Automobile Indus-

try Introduction," Plunkett Research, http://www.plunkettre
search.com/automobiles%20trucks%20market%20research/in
dustry%20overview.

167 **a transfer of $325 billion to foreign governments:** The U.S.
Energy Information Administration estimates that in 2010 the
United States imported 4,289,772,000 barrels of oil at an average
price of $75.87 per barrel; http://www.eia.gov/.

169 **Leaf, launched in 2011 with a retail price of $33,000:** Camille
Ricketts, "Nissan Leaf Undercuts Rivals with $33,000 Price Tag,"
VentureBeat.com, March 30, 2010, http://venturebeat.com/2010/
03/30/nissan-leaf-undercuts-rivals-with-33000-price-tag/. For the
2012 model year, Nissan raised the price of the base model to
$35,200.

169 **Versa can travel over 400 miles on a full tank of gas:** Steve Almasy,
"The New Fear: Electric Car 'Range Anxiety,'" *CNN.com,* October 20,
2010, http://www.cnn.com/2010/US/10/18/ev.charging.stations/
index.html.

169 **Most drives are well within this range:** "Average Annual Miles per
Driver per Age Group," U.S. Department of Transporation Federal
Highway Administration, http://www.fhwa.dot.gov/ohim/onh00/
bar8.htm. Accessed August 4, 2011.

170 **3,834 public charge stations deployed across 39 states:** "Alternative Fueling Station Total Counts by State and Fuel Type," U.S.
Department of Energy, http://www.afdc.energy.gov/afdc/fuels/
stations_counts.html. Accessed October 23, 2011.

171 **Drivers reaching the end of their battery power:** The range of
the Volt is 25 to 50 miles, depending on temperature, terrain, and
driving style, before the gas generator kicks in. Essentially, this
means that even if you drive 60 miles per day, you get an unheard-of
150 miles per gallon.

171 **Volt is an expensive proposition at $41,000:** Nick Bunkley, "The
Volt, G.M.'s Plug-In Car, Gets a $41,000 Price Tag," *New York Times,*
July 27, 2010.

171 **similarly equipped Chevrolet Cruze:** Terry Box, "A Cruze Worth Taking," *Dallas Morning News,* November 20, 2010.

171 **"But do I think it's going to be a volume seller? No":** Jonathan Welsh, "Chevy Volt: Are Electric Cars Too Expensive?," *Wall Street Journal,* July 28, 2010.

171 **"pitching these products only to the rich":** Daniel Gross, "The Volt Jolt," *Slate.com,* July 28, 2010.

173 **key component of a new car's value and attractiveness:** "2011 Best New Car Values: Best Resale Value," Kiplinger.com. Accessed June 9, 2011.

174 **750-megawatt load:** 24 kWh battery charged over 8 hours draws 3 kW continuously for the charge cycle; 3 kW × 250,000 cars = 750-MW load.

174 **L.A. County's average electric load:** According to the California Energy Commision, Los Angeles Country consumed a total of 73,089.6 million kWh in 2009. Dividing by 365 days/year, 24 hours/day, and 1,000 kw/MW yields an average consumption load of 8,344 MW. See http://ecdms.energy.ca.gov/elecbycounty.aspx.

180 **"no other job could compare":** Josette Akresh-Gonzales, "Energy CEO Shai Agassi on Recognizing a 'Sliding Doors' Moment," *Harvard Business Review,* May 1, 2009.

184 **placed an order for 100,000 Fluence Z.E. cars:** Jim Motavalli, "Better Place Reveals E.V. Charging Plan and Customer Center in Denmark," *New York Times,* March 4, 2011.

186 **"It's MY car, MY battery, and MY time":** Reader comment posted in response to Jeff St. John, "Electric Vehicles Could Surpass Grid or Support It," *GreentechMedia.com,* May 28, 2009, http://www .greentechmedia.com/articles/read/electric-vehicles-could-surpass-grid-or-support-it/.

187 **a more detailed analysis:** This is a scenario for thinking about relative prices. The key here is the logic rather than the specific values, all of which are reasonable as of the time of this writing, but which are also subject to change as a function of

technological advance, bargaining power, geopolitics, tax regimes, etc.

The cost of an e-mile consists of:

Electricity cost: $0.025/mile (at $0.10 per kWh—the industrial rate in Israel and Denmark; in the United States it is less than $0.07—and 4 miles per kWh). Note that as technology improves and the number of miles per kWh rises, this cost will decrease.

Battery cost: $0.06/mile (at $650/kWh capacity, 24 kWh capacity, and a usable battery life of 250,000 miles). Note that improvements in batteries are sure to decrease cost per kWh and increase battery life.

Infrastructure cost: This cost is highly dependent on the number of charge spots and change stations to be deployed, their functional life span, the number of drivers, and the average number of miles driven. For an early market, a rough estimate—mine, not the company's—might be $0.03 per mile ($200 million expenditure, lasting 10 years, for 40,000 drivers, driving 15,000 miles per year). This cost will decrease as additional drivers use the fixed infrastructure.

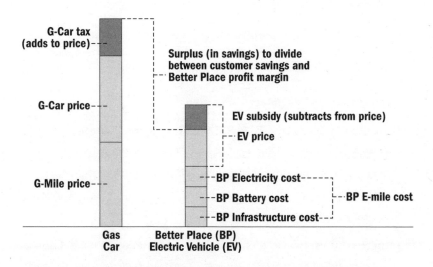

Figure N.1: The determinants of economic advantage for the Better Place model.

In this scenario (you can play with numbers as you wish), the cost to Better Place of an e-mile is $0.105. If one were to factor in government direct and indirect subsidies for infrastructure, the tax benefits that come from being able to depreciate the value of both the batteries and infrastructure, etc., this number can be substantially lower (and it probably is).

The price of a g-mile depends on two things: the price of a gallon of gas, and the mileage it yields. A typical mid-sized car might average 30 miles per gallon. But there is no such thing as a typical gas price. Although there is a global price of oil, gas prices vary dramatically across regions depending on tax policies. In July of 2011, for example, the average price of a gallon of gas was $3.58 in the United States, $8.33 in Israel, and $8.87 in Denmark. And so the price of a g-mile was $0.13 in the United States, $0.30 in Israel, and $0.32. At these prices, there are no savings in the United States, but at 15,000 miles per year, the annual savings in Denmark are $3,225 in Denmark and $2,925 in Israel. Over four years, this amounts to $12,900 and $11,700 respectively.

188 **conventional cars are taxed at 180 percent, EVs at 0 percent:** Daniel Roth, "Driven: Shai Agassi's Audacious Plan to Put Electric Cars on the Road," *Wired,* August 18, 2008.

188 **one of the most environmentally conscious countries:** Nelson Schwartz, "In Denmark, Ambitious Plan for Electric Cars," *New York Times,* December 1, 2009.

188 **fewer than 500 registered EVs:** Ibid.

188 **purchase a Fluence Z.E. at $37,962:** European Commission Competition, "Car Prices Within the European Union," January 1, 2010.

188 **investors who have entrusted over $700 million:** Nelson Schwartz, "Sites to Recharge Cars Gain a Big Dose of Funds," *New York Times,* January 25, 2010.

189 **successful network technologies of yesteryear:** See Thomas Parker Hughes, *Networks of Power: Electrification in Western Society,*

1880–1930 (Baltimore, Md.: Johns Hopkins University Press, 1983), for a fascinating history.

[CHAPTER 8]

195 **65 percent of the Kenyan population:** "In Rural Kenya, M-Pesa Is Used as a Savings Account Tool," *Mobile Payment Magazine,* March 3, 2011.

195 **81 percent of Kenyans did not have access to a bank account:** "Enabling Mobile Money Transfer: The Central Bank of Kenya's Treatment of M-Pesa," *Alliance for Financial Inclusion,* case study, 2010, p. 2.

195 **27 percent of its citizens owned mobile phones:** Ibid., p. 92.

195 **63 percent of Kenyans were mobile phone subscribers:** Kachwanya, "Kenyan Mobile Phone Penetration Is Now over 63%," June 7, 2011. Data in figure 4, "Mobile Penetration," provided by Communications Commission of Kenya. http://www.kach wanya.com/ 2011/06/07/kenyan-mobile-phone-penetration-is-now-over-63/. Accessed August 2, 2011. See also http: //mobilemonday.co.ke/ page/2/.

196 **"too many challenges to mention":** Jaco Maritz, "Exclusive Interview: The Woman Behind M-PESA," *How We Made It in Africa,* November 11, 2010, http://www.howwemadeitinafrica.com/exclu sive-interview-the-woman-behind-m-pesa/5496/.

197 **considerable complexity was added:** Sarah Rotman, "M-PESA: A Very Simple and Secure Customer Proposition," *CGAP.org,* November 5, 2008, http://technology.cgap.org/2008/11/05/m-pesa-a-very-simple-and-secure-customer-proposition/.

197 **"bottleneck in transferring the money":** Nick Hughes and Susie Lonie, "M-PESA: Mobile Money for the 'Unbanked'—Turning Cellphones into 24-Hour Tellers in Kenya," *Innovations,* Winter/ Spring 2007, p. 77.

198 **"we would need to find a way to simplify things":** Ibid., p. 74.

200 **expanded its customer base to 7.3 million:** Michael Ouma, "M-Pesa Now Ventures Abroad to Tap into Diaspora Cash," *East African,* October 19, 2009, http://www.theeastafrican.co.ke/busi ness/-/2560/673512/-/5gaimnz/-/index.html.

201 **(Kenya's GDP in 2009 was $63 billion):** CIA World Factbook, https://www.cia.gov/library/publications/the-world-factbook/ geos/ke.html. Accessed July 15, 2011.

201 **"no Kenyan is locked out of accessing basic banking services":** "M-Kesho: 'Super Bank Account' from Safaricom and Equity Bank," Techmtaa.com, May 18, 2010, http://www.techmtaa.com/ 2010/05/18/m-kesho-super-bank-account-from-safaricom-and- equity-bank/.

207 **"Creative Zen Vision:M certainly has the goods":** "CNET Editors Cover the Best of CES 2006," *CNET.com,* http://www.cnet.com/ 4520-11405_1-6398234-1.html.

207 **"hand-held computer that's fully in the iPhone's class":** Walt Mossberg, "Palm's New Pre Takes On iPhone," *Wall Street Journal,* June 3, 2009.

207 **"the Android tablet concept":** David Pogue, "It's a Tablet. It's Gorgeous. It's Costly," *New York Times,* November 10, 2010.

209 **90 percent of the world that used Windows:** Ian Fried, "Are Mac Users Smarter?" *CNET.com,* July 12, 2002, http://news.cnet.com/ 2100-1040-943519.html.

210 **iPod, boasting 100 million customers:** Steven Levy, "Why We Went Nuts About the iPhone," *Newsweek,* July 16, 2007.

210 **Apple's stock shot up 44 percent:** Matt Krantz, "iPhone Powers up Apple's Shares," *USA Today,* June 28, 2007.

211 **"four times the number of PCs that ship every year":** Morris, "Steve Jobs Speaks Out."

211 **Ericsson released the R380:** Dave Conabree, "Ericsson Introduces the New R380e," *Mobile Magazine,* September 25, 2001.

211 **Palm followed up with its version:** Sascha Segan, "Kyocera Launches First Smartphone in Years," *PC Magazine,* March 23, 2010, http://www.pcmag.com/article2/0,2817,2361664,00.asp#fbid =C81SVwKJIvh.

211 **"one more entrant into an already very busy space":** "RIM Co-CEO Doesn't See Threat from Apple's iPhone," *InformationWeek,* February 12, 2007.

212 **the phone was exclusively available from only one carrier:** In a handful of markets regulators ruled the exclusivity arrangement illegal.

212 **"The bigger problem is the AT&T network":** David Pogue, "The iPhone Matches Most of Its Hype," *New York Times,* June 27, 2007.

212 **priced at a mere $99 in 2007:** Kim Hart, "Rivals Ready for iPhone's Entrance; Pricey Gadget May Alter Wireless Field," *Washington Post,* June 24, 2007.

212 **"cause irreparable damage to the iPhone's software":** Apple, press release, September 24, 2007.

213 **"I say I like our strategy":** Steve Ballmer interviewed on CNBC, January 17, 2007.

213 **They ran out of the older model six weeks before the July 2008 launch:** Tom Krazit, "The iPhone, One Year Later," *CNET.com,* June 26, 2008, http://news.cnet.com/8301-13579_3-9977572-37 .html.

213 **60 percent went to buyers who already owned at least one iPod:** Apple COO Tim Cook's comments at Goldman Sachs Technology and Internet Conference, cited in JPMorgan analyst report, "Strolling Through the Apple Orchard: The Good, the Bad and the Ugly Scenarios," March 4, 2008.

215 **the average iPhone user paid AT&T $2,000:** Jenna Wortham, "Customers Angered as iPhones Overload AT&T," *New York Times,* September 2, 2009.

215 **as high as $18 per user per month:** Tom Krazit, "Piper Jaffray: AT&T Paying Apple $18 per iPhone, Per Month," *CNET.com,* October 24, 2007, http://news.cnet.com/8301-13579_3-9803657-37 .html.

216 **Apple announced its 10 billionth app download:** Apple.com, "iTunes Store Tops 10 Billion Songs Sold," February 25, 2010, http://www.apple.com/pr/library/2010/02/25iTunes-Store-Tops-10-Billion-Songs-Sold.html. Accessed October 20, 2011.

219 **financial analysts, technology blogs, and the mainstream media were already obsessed:** James Quinn, "Apple's 'Tablet' to rival Amazon's Kindle," *Daily Telegraph* (London), May 22, 2009.

219 **"Apple's latest billion-dollar jackpot":** David Smith, "Steve Jobs' New Trick: The Apple Tablet," *Observer,* August 23, 2009.

219 **"2010 Could be the Year of the Tablet":** Nick Bilton, "2010 Could be the Year of the Tablet," *New York Times,* December 28, 2009.

219 **"already 75 million people who know how to use this":** Joshua Topolosky, "Live from the Apple 'Latest Creation' Event," *Engadget .com,* January 27, 2010.

219 **all committed to providing books for the device:** Ibid.

219 **daily version of the paper specially tailored for iPad users:** Andy Brett, "The New York Times Introduces an iPad App," *TechCrunch,* April 1, 2010, http://techcrunch.com/2010/04/01/new-york-times-ipad/. Accessed July 24, 2011.

219 **Rupert Murdoch even created an iPad-only newspaper:** Dylan Stableford and Tim Molloy, "Rupert Murdoch Launches His iPad-Only Newspaper," *Wrap,* February 2, 2011.

219 **Condé Nast created iPad-only digital versions:** Stephanie Clifford, "Condé Nast Is Preparing iPad Versions of Some of Its Top Magazines," *New York Times,* February 28, 2010.

219 **"we are committing the resources necessary":** Ibid.

220 **asymmetric risk:** Ron Adner and William Vincent, "iPad: A Dubious Bet for Publishers," *Forbes.com,* November 29, 2010; http://

www.forbes.com/2010/11/29/apple-ipad-publishers-leadership
-managing-magazines.html. Accessed October 23, 2011.

221 **public fallouts:** Georgina Prodhan, "*Financial Times* Pulls Its Apps
from Apple Store," Reuters, August 31, 2011; http://www.reuters
.com/article/2011/08/31/us-apple-ft-idUSTRE77U1O020110831.
Accessed October 23, 2011.

221 **"Economically untenable":** Julianne Pepitone, "Rhapsody: Apple
Has Gone Too Far," *CNNMoney*, February 16, 2011; http://money.
cnn.com/2011/02/16/technology/rhapsody_apple_subscrip
tions/index.htm.

222 **poster child was Canon:** C. K. Prahalad and Gary Hamel, "The
Core Competence of the Corporation," *Harvard Business Review*,
May 1, 1990.

INDEX